THEOLOGY AND TECHNOLOGY, *VOLUME 1*

Theology and Technology, *Volume 1*

Essays in Christian Analysis

Edited by Carl Mitcham, Jim Grote,
and Levi Checketts

WIPF & STOCK · Eugene, Oregon

THEOLOGY AND TECHNOLOGY, VOLUME 1
Essays in Christian Analysis

Wipf & Stock
An Imprint of Wipf and Stock Publishers
199 W. 8th Ave., Suite 3
Eugene, OR 97401

www.wipfandstock.com

PAPERBACK ISBN: 978-1-6667-3462-1
HARDCOVER ISBN: 978-1-6667-9068-9
EBOOK ISBN: 978-1-6667-9069-6

JULY 14, 2022 9:53 AM

Originally published as *Theology and Technology: Essays in Christian Analysis and Exegesis*
Copyright: 1984
Lanham: University Press of America

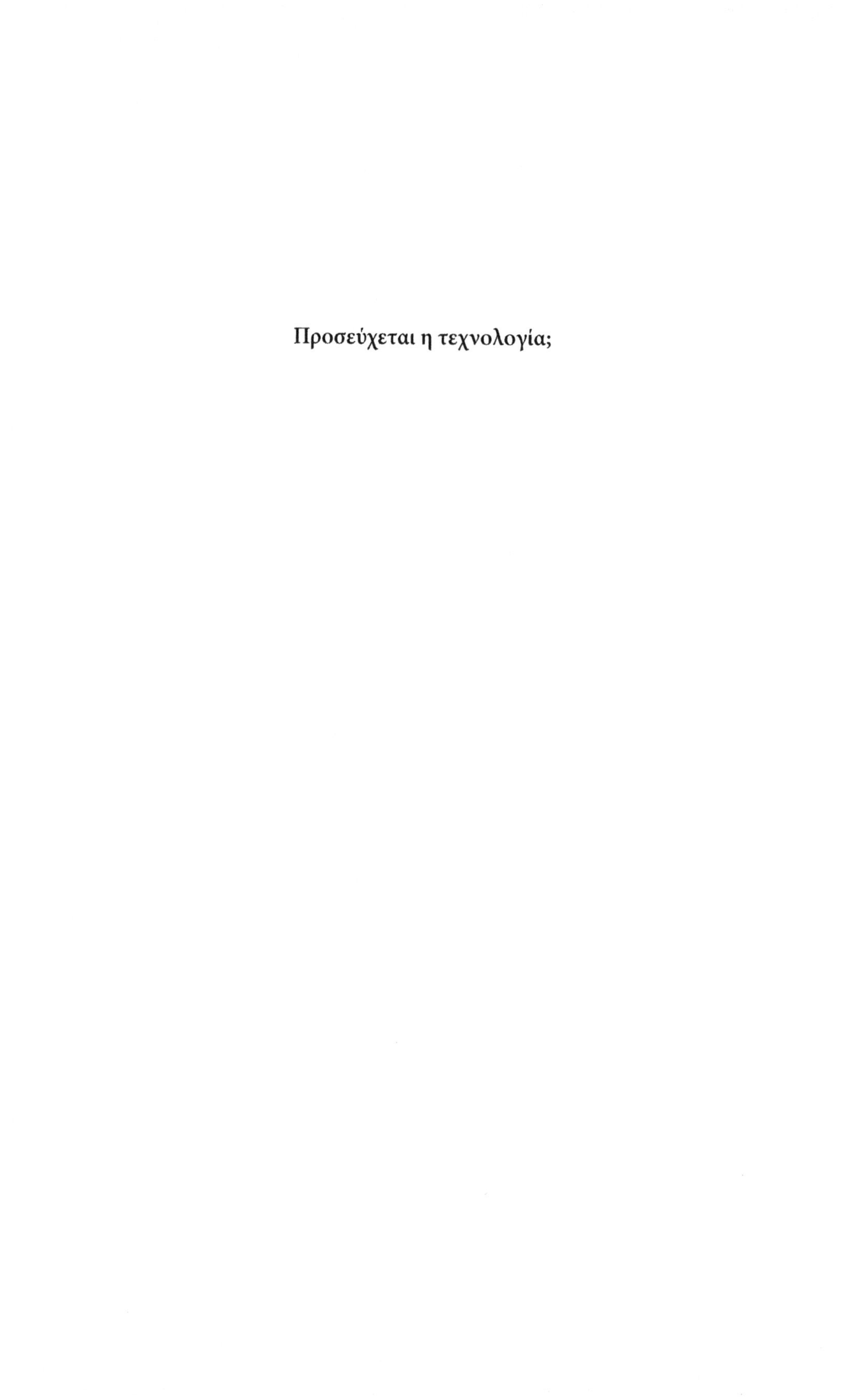

Προσεύχεται η τεχνολογία;

Contents

Contributors

Note: The biographical notes, with the exception of the addition of Levi Checketts, are from the original publication. It seemed appropriate to leave them in this form, as indices to the author careers at the time they wrote. I note only the passing of four contributors: George A. Blair (1934–2013), Wilhelm E. Fudpucker (1923–2008), Jim Grote (1954–2013), Andre Malet (1919–1989), and Terry Tekippe (1940–2005). *Requiescat in Pace.*

George A. Blair is Professor of Philosophy and Chairman of the Philosophy Department at Thomas More College, Kentucky, where he has been teaching for eighteen years. He received his Master's Degree in Philosophy from Boston College, and his Doctorate from Fordham University, and at one time was a Fulbright Exchange Teacher in Argentina. In his early years, he was in the Jesuit Seminary in the New England Province of that order, but left before becoming a priest.

Levi Checketts is an Assistant Professor of Religion and Philosophy at Hong Kong Baptist University. While unable to call one locale his hometown, he has lived the majority of his life in the Western US, from the deserts of Utah and Nevada to the evergreen hills of Oregon and the Northern California coast. He completed his PhD in Christian Ethics at the Graduate Theological Union in 2018, articulating a constructive moral anthropology for new technologies entitled *Homo gubernator: A Moral Anthropology for New Technologies*. Prior to his post in Hong Kong, he taught at Holy Names University in Oakland, Santa Clara University and St Mary's College of California. He is currently working on a monograph critiquing the epistemological aims of Artificial Intelligence through a hermeneutic of poverty.

Wilhelm E. Fudpucker was born April 10, 1923, in Fredericksburg, Texas, of German immigrant parents. His father was associated with Ernst Kapp and the Texas Hegelians. He first studied physics at the California Institute of Technology, and then in 1942 followed J. Robert Oppenheimer to Los Alamos, New Mexico. After the war he returned to Texas and worked in Lyndon Johnson's 1948 campaign for the U.S. Senate. Later he met Fr. Pierre Teilhard de Chardin in New York, and when Teilhard died on Easter Sunday, 1955, Fudpucker says that he had "a religious experience which eventually led me to join the Jesuits," He has since returned to Germany and the Massenheim Institute, where his research centers around physics, evolutionary theory, Heidegger, and politics. His major work is *The Shepherd of Becoming* (London: Noosphere Press, 1978).

Jim Grote, born July 15, 1953, in Louisville, Kentucky, received his M.A. in philosophy from the University of Louisville. He has been a Lecturer in Philosophy at St. Catharine College (Kentucky), the University of Louisville, and Indiana University Southeast. He has contributed reviews, editorial, and bibliographic work to Research in Philosophy and Technology. He is married, has one child, and is currently working for the St. Vincent de Paul Society.

André Malet is Professor on the Faculté des Sciences Humaines at the Université de Dijon. He holds Doctorates in theology and in political science from the Sorbonne. His books include *Personne et amour dans la theologie trinitaire de S. Thomas D'Aquin* (Paris: Vrin, 1956); *Jean Calvin, Commentaire sur la Genèse: Texte etabli par A. Malet* (Geneva: Labor et Fides, 1962); *Le Traité théologique-politique de Spinoza et la pensée biblique* (Paris: Belles Lettres, 1966); and *The Thought of Rudolf Bultmann* (Garden City, NY: Doubleday, 1971).

Carl Mitcham has had a checkered academic career. He was born (1941) and raised in Dallas, Texas; did formal studies at the University of Colorado and Stanford University, and informal studies at a number of other institutions; held teaching positions at Berea College and St. Catharine College (both of Kentucky); and is currently at the Polytechnic Institute of New York in Brooklyn. For nine years he and his wife and four children were involved in an experiment in contemplative family community. His published works include *Philosophy and Technology*, edited with Robert Mackey (New York: Free Press, 1972; paper back reprint, 1983); *Bibliography of the Philosophy of Technology*, again co-authored with Mackey

(Chicago: University of Chicago Press, 1973); and the "Philosophy of Technology" chapter in Paul Durbin, ed., *Guide to the Culture of Science, Technology, and Medicine* (New York: Free Press, 1980).

Following in the tradition of Herman Dooyeweerd (1894–1977) and Hendrick van Riessen (born 1911), **Egbert Schuurman** (born 1937) is a representative of the third generation of Dutch neo-Calvinist philosophers. He has Doctorates in engineering as well as philosophy and holds a joint appointment at the Technical Universities of Delft and Eindhoven and at the Free University of Amsterdam. His works in English include *Reflections on the Technological Society* (Toronto: Wedge Publishing Foundation, 1977) and *Technology and the Future: A Philosophical Challenge* (Toronto: Wedge, 1980).

Terry J, Tekippe was born in Cedar Rapids, Iowa, in 1940. He did theological studies at the Gregorian University in Rome, and was ordained a priest of the (Roman Catholic) Archdiocese of New Orleans in 1965. He has Doctorates in both theology (Fordham University, 1972) and philosophy (Tulane, 1980). Currently he does teaching and research at St. Joseph's Seminary in New Orleans. During 1977 and 1978 he lived at Open House Community, a family religious center in Lake Charles, Louisiana; he is an airplane pilot; and he spent the summer of 1982 studying in Japan. His book *Christian Living Today* was published by Paulist Press in 1978. Co-editor of the *Lonergan Studies Newsletter*, he has recently edited and contributed to *Papal Infallibility: An Application of Lonergan's Theological Method* (Washington, DC: University Press of America, 1983).

Foreword (2022)

On Republishing *Theology and Technology*

LEVI CHECKETTS

THIS BOOK IS a revised reprinting of Carl Mitcham and Jim Grote's 1984 *Theology and Technology: Essays in Christian Analysis and Exegesis*. As Mitcham explains in his concluding essay, this work grew out of interest in expanding the field of philosophy of technology to theology. Theology and philosophy, after all, have been companion disciplines, mutually influencing each other in a formal way since Medieval Europeans began creating universities nearly one thousand years ago, but have complemented each other in a much less formal way across continents (Europe, Africa and Asia) since ancient thinkers like Plato, Confucius and Siddhartha Gautama lived and taught. It is only appropriate, then, that, as philosophy and technology grew, so too should theological studies of technology. Mitcham's interest in the subject, growing out of his founding role in the Society for Philosophy and Technology and his work on the earlier *Philosophy and Technology: Readings in the Philosophical Problems of Technology*, resulted in collaboration with Jim Grote to put this work together.

When I began my own PhD studies at the Graduate Theological Union, I knew already that my focus would be Christian ethics of new technologies. I had been interested in technologies from childhood, likely influenced too much by science-fiction movies and TV. In my master's studies, I saw how inundated were fields of applied Christians ethics like bioethics and just war and knew my own personal limitations when it came to topics like sexual and racial justice. Technological ethics seemed a natural fit, but I found it difficult to situate my work given that, as far as I was able to discover, the field did not seem to exist.

I discovered this text quite serendipitously. In doing preliminary reading for comprehensive examinations, I read Ian Barbour's *Ethics in an Age of Technology*, the second volume of his Gifford Lectures (the first being *Religion in an Age of Science*). Barbour, like Mitcham, saw a parallel that needed addressing, but whereas Mitcham went from philosophy and technology to theology and technology, Barbour went from theology and science to ethics and technology. Also like Mitcham, this part of Barbour's work is less well-known than his main area of writing. Barbour begins his *Ethics in an Age of Technology* by providing a genealogy of the field, a lineage which includes rather obscure texts like Victor Ferkiss's 1969 *Technological Man* or David Kipnis's 1990 *Technology and Power* as well as the more renowned work of Jacques Ellul. Barbour very positively cites Mitcham and Grote's volume as an important resource for contextualizing and framing theological questions of technology.

I was quite lucky to find a copy of Mitcham and Grote's work at the Graduate Theological Union library, but, to my surprise, it had not been checked out in over *two decades*. (This was surprising because the GTU is home to the Center for Theology and Natural Sciences, which Barbour helped found.) A year later, I taught a course to master's students at the GTU and included *Theology and Technology* as a primary text. We read the methodological essays (Volume I) in parallel with contemporary scholarship from Science and Technology Studies (STS) scholars and philosophers of technology. We read the chapters on exegesis and historical perspectives (Volume II) alongside history of technology papers. We read the analysis essays (Volume II) along with essays from Karl Rahner, Thomas Merton, Wendell Berry, and Paul Tillich. The students found the engagement with the 1984 text alongside others to be rewarding and stimulating. But they all lamented one thing: the text was not easy to acquire. It was almost entirely absent from second-hand bookstores and copies on the Internet sometimes had price tags of $200 or more! Needless to say, this was quite prohibitive for my students in obtaining their own copies!

It is with great joy that I have the privilege of reprinting this in collaboration with Carl Mitcham and the support of the International Jacques Ellul Society. It is regrettable that most of the original authors, including Mitcham's original co-editor Jim Grote, have already passed on and are thus unable to offer reflections or comments about this reprinting. Nonetheless, it is the hope of all of us involved in this process that this republication will serve current and future generations of students by, at the very least, making these essays more affordable and accessible to the average reader.

Critical need for reading these texts

The field of theological studies of technology, as is true for its more specific but more practical subfield of theological ethics of technology, has been subject to many false starts. Mitcham and Grote hoped to spur a conversation with this text in 1984, but complications and loss of interest from other parties stymied any greater development. A few years later, Ian Barbour lectured on theological ethics of technology in his Gifford Lectures, but he was unable to garner the same interest in this subject that theology and science gained. In 2010, the *Journal of Religion, Theology and Technology*, an offshoot from *Zygon: Journal of Religion and Science*, debuted, but produced only eight articles across two years before shutting down.

Above all else, one only need look at the list of books of theologians who wrote on technology to never return to the subject, such as Norman Faramelli (*Technethics*, 1971) who is most known for his economic and ecological work, Paul Tillich (*The Spiritual Situation in Our Technical Society*, 1988) who is most well-known for his existentialist theology, and James Gustafson ("Christian Attitudes toward a Technological Society," 1959) whose work focuses on fundamental moral theology. This field lacks the lifelong commitments that philosophy of technology has held. We have no figures to date who span decades and generations of thought like Carl Mitcham, Don Ihde, Albert Borgmann or Andrew Feenberg. No professional society exists for this field, and the senior scholars who do write on the subject, are often too diffuse in their focus, often focusing on science, technology, theology and ethics in a general way (with a greater general interest in theology and science above all else).

The present moment, however, offers an important opportunity to try once again. Over the past decade, greater and greater interest has grown in theological studies of technology. New conferences have emerged, including TheoCom Conference on Theology and Digital Media, starting in 2012 and sponsored in part by the United States Conference of Catholic Bishops and the Ecumenical Patriarchate of the Greek Orthodox Diocese of America; the Jesuit Seminar on Religion and Technology, run by Tim Clancy, SJ from Gonzaga University; and devoted annual sessions of the

Pacific Coast Theological Society's meetings (notably Fall 2020 and Fall 2017). New non-profit organizations have emerged, such as TheoTech, an eschatologically-oriented NGO focused on using digital technology to usher in God's reign, founded in 2013; FaithTech, a similar organization with greater focus on general evangelization, founded in 2016; AI and Faith, devoted to interreligious conversations around Artificial Intelligence, founded in 2018; and AI Theology, a growing organization focused exclusively on Christian theological approaches to AI, founded in 2017. New research centers have emerged, including the Carl G. Greffenstette Center for Ethics in Science, Technology and Law at Duquesne University, opened in 2020; the Technology Ethics Center sponsored by IBM at the University of Notre Dame, opened in 2019; and the Center for Ethics and Transformative Technologies sponsored by Microsoft at Seattle University, also opened in 2019. Even a "Digital Theology" master's program is offered by Spurgeon's College in the United Kingdom (previously by Durham University).

This moment is a critical point for the possibility of truly establishing a field of theological studies of technology. The field does not yet enjoy the recognition of more established sub-areas of theology, such as biomedical ethics, theology and science, or Christian spirituality. Its fits and starts have resulted in a lack of central discussion surrounding the important work done in this area, and the enthusiasm of scholars in the field is beginning to flag. As new scholars arise, they are not engaging with fundamental or grounding texts; when I have refereed articles for *Theology and Science*, *The Journal of Moral Theology* or other journals, I am surprised how little attention aspiring scholars give to questions of theory or method. The Digital Theology program of Spurgeon's College is taught by faculty members who ran the program at Durham; it is not a "new" program but a transfer of an existing one. TheoCom and the Jesuit Seminar for Religion and Technology held no conferences in 2021, though this may be in part due to the COVID 19 pandemic.

In short, if there *is* to be a theological studies of technology—and not merely a continuation of passing fascinations with the topic—the time is now. The current energy and financial support behind such efforts should be harnessed, but, more critically, the scholastic interest should not be left to cool. Technological changes persist, and theology is woefully behind in addressing them. On the other hand, theology is a subject the success of which is increasingly precarious, and yet is all the more necessary as technological values take over society. If theological studies of technology does not materialize soon, it may never get its chance.

There is no reason to take the present work as *the* definitive volume for theological studies of technology. A new collection may be organized, such as the 2020 book *Theology and Technology*, edited by William H. U. Anderson, or another collection of older works might be assembled that includes older theologians such as Jürgen Moltmann, Willem B. Drees and Pierre Teilhard de Chardin. My hope in reprinting *this* collection is to offer *some* starting point for present and future generations of theologians, and what better place to start than an effort intentionally taken to this end. If this work only serves to underscore, for example, the importance of Jacques Ellul, Carl Mitcham and Albert Borgmann for future theological considerations, it will be successful in its endeavor.

My greater hope, however, is this work will provide a foundation for future programs and theological developments, providing not a limit for thought, but a shared basis from which theologians studying technology might dialogue. The methodological essays in the first volume are essential for thinking through the way theologians have and continue to address technology as a phenomenon, and they helpfully conclude with new directions to consider. The essays of the second volume provide starting points for students of various branches of theology, from biblical studies in the first part, to historical reflections in the second part, and contemporary engagements in the final section. The variety of critical theological reflections represented in these pages offer any student or scholar a wealth of material from which to begin or hone her own theological engagement with technologies. These essays represent, above all, a *starting* place, an origin of thinking about technology that could foreground our present and future reflection. It is my hope that contemporary and later generations of scholars move beyond the views expressed here. But in going *beyond*, it is important to first know what has gone *before*.

Some notes on language

At the time this work was originally published, academic theology reinscribed, as it does still today, many of the biases of its time. As such, an astute reader will note that absent from this work women, LGBTQ perspectives, nearly any persons of color, or non-western voices. Indeed, as Carl Mitcham and I began discussion of republishing this volume, he noted this as the major shortcoming of the original text. A hope we both share is that this work can spur and inspire the critical response of under-represented voices. Such efforts exist, such as the Ecclesia for Women in Asia's *Feminist Cyberethics in Asia: Religious Discourses on Human Connectivity* (2014) or Philip Butler's *Black Transhuman Liberation Theology: Technology and Spirituality* (2019), and other texts noted in the conclusion to Volume I. We are grateful for the work already existent on this front and look forward to continuing critical engagements from scholars not representing hegemonic voices.

I recognize, then, that this book has blind spots in its range of perspectives, its language, its assumptions about the world, and its engagement with the realities of persons who are not white, cis-gendered, heterosexual Christian males. The omission of diverse voices was an oversight, but that oversight represents the problem of "blindness" inherent in hegemonic perspectives. Nonetheless, I hope contemporary readers recognize in good faith the need to pick up where these texts left off and carry on the conversation in new directions. I hope that current and future scholars will engage these essays with critique, response, and reflection. In line with Martin Heidegger, whose thought is both controversial because of his Nazism, and important because of its contributions to philosophy, especially philosophy of technology, I note that "We have been a conversation."[1] The conversation should not stop with this book but be carried on by those who go forward.

I must therefore further note many of the essays in these volume contain language which reflects an "old boys" style of academic writing. The word "man," for example, is used almost exclusively as a substitute for "humanity" or "the human." There are other turns of phrase or expressions which betray a Western/Eurocentric and masculine paradigm. Christian Supersessionism runs rampant in some of the essays. Anti-Semitism, Islamophobia and anti-Orientalist positions are implied and sometimes stated. Ableism is noticeable in some of the essays. I had the option of editing out some of this language in this reprint but kept it for two reasons: first, I believe that, as noted above, it is important for current and future scholars to be able to grapple with these essays critically. Censoring or editing these would be more palatable for readers, but it denies the historical reality of the development of thought. I ask contemporary

1. Heidegger, "Hölderlin and the Essence of Poetry," 121.

readers to engage this with the same recognition of its merits and critique of its shortcomings as we might any other theological or academic text generated in the same period. Moreover, being able to see the shortcomings gives us room to reflect on how the conversations surrounding theology and technology has remained myopic. Second, I recognize it is not my place to decide whether the authors "really meant" something else. Most of the authors of this work have already passed on, and it is not my interest, nor is it appropriate for me, to speak on their behalf. Reading is itself an interpretive practice; the author has no control of how the reader interprets their work. Moreover, it may not even be for the author to decide what they "really meant."[2] As such, I leave the text as is, with only corrections of spelling, grammar, punctuation, and formatting.

Outline of work

In the process of deciding how to reprint this work, we have taken the original *Theology and Technology* and made some changes. The most significant change is the decision to break the single work into two separate volumes the first oriented around questions of method, and the second around specific theological perspectives. This follows the division Mitcham and Grote outline in their original work, with the essays of Part I of their work corresponding primarily with Volume I, and the essays of the three sections of Part II in Volume II.

The original text also contained a lengthy annotated bibliography spanning from pages 325 to 502 inclusive. Mitcham and I agree this is an invaluable reference, but it is omitted for two reasons: first, the bibliography itself has not been updated faithfully since 1984 and so lacks any of the important recent texts on the subject; second, we agreed an online bibliography, which is anticipated to be hosted on the International Jacques Ellul Society's website, would prove more valuable since it can easily be updated for new works and more accessible to broader audiences.

One final change is noted: in addition to this new preface, Volume I also contains three new additions, an essay from me, a retrospective from Mitcham, and a new conclusion to parallel this foreword. The essays in

2. As Hans Jonas puts it, "Nothing, neither experience nor good sense, supports the view that the author is his own best interpreter." Jonas, "Change and Permanence," 252.

Volume II, except for the new foreword, are all essays originally published in the first edition, though the division of the volume differs slightly from its original structure.

Volume I begins with an essay from Carl Mitcham outlining the basic questions of approach to theological studies of technology. Mitcham summarizes the views of the following five essays and conceptually ties them to H. Richard Niebuhr's *Christ and Culture* typology. Mitcham notes the ways these essays reinforce or follow one ideal type over other alternative approaches, sometimes more faithfully and sometimes less so. Mitcham concludes that while Niebuhr doesn't give preference for one model over another, Christians should adopt an antagonistic or tense attitude toward technology because of its threat to the singular focus Christianity calls us to.

The five essays which follow Mitcham's are a variety of original and duplicated essays which correspond to these ideal types. George Blair's short essay articulates a position for the Christian outside of technology. His main point is not that technology is evil, but rather that it leads us to questions and concerns which distract us from Christian living. Wilhelm Fudpucker's bombastic essay takes the opposite tack, underscoring the importance of technology for Christian goals through the thought of two important Jesuits: Pierre Teilhard de Chardin and Walter Ong. A third Jesuit is added to this count in Terry Tekippe's essay on Bernard Lonergan. While Lonergan said little about technology, Tekippe adapts what Lonergan wrote about science and argues that Lonergan's position is essentially a dualistic one—technology is neither opposed to Christianity nor inherently good for it. André Malet's essay draws heavily from Heidegger's philosophy of technology and the dangers that technological thinking presents, but he notes that the moral task of building the Kingdom of God can redirect the otherwise dangerous tendencies that technologies present. Finally, Egbert Schuurman takes a "transformative" view and places his thinking in contrast to that of Jacques Ellul: while he accepts that the motivations of technology are destructive, he argues that technology subjected to Christian motivations is good.

Volume I concludes with two brand new essays. The first is my own, proposing a new direction for theological studies of technology drawing insight from STS. I argue that the histories of Christian theology and technology suggest a more dialectical relationship between the two spheres—not one of separation but of mutual co-construction. The second essay is a retrospective from Mitcham about the process that went into creating this work originally and his own theological journey from when it was published to present. Mitcham reiterates his oppositionist stance, but suggests that Christianity may actually be unable to maintain such a position. We conclude this essay with an interview between Mitcham and me, opening new directions with Chinese religion and technology. The conclusion to this volume offers no new arguments but frames new directions for both Christian theological studies of technology and further religious engagements that are in dire need.

Volume II opens with an essay from the original co-editors, Carl Mitcham and Jim Grote. This essay introduces the works of the volume and outlines them according to a framework of hermeneutics and the theological virtues. Like Mitcham's introductory essay in Volume I, this essay serves both to introduce to the reader the content of the second volume and to articulate the authors' own theological position. Mitcham and Grote first note the inherently intertwined nature of hermeneutics and technology, both historically and in modern developments of the field. They then critique inappropriate attitudes toward technology that co-opt the theological virtues of faith, hope and charity, and offer an appraisal of the theological virtues apart from technology.

The three essays following this, under Part I of Volume II, are broadly concerned with biblical readings of technology. The section opens with two essays from Jacques Ellul, who reflects on the way God's good creation contradicts *technique*'s drive to mastery over all, and ponders the reality of our lapsarian condition in light of *technique*. Charles Mabee's essay challenges the American mythological hermeneutic, one characterized by an elevation of technological progress, as being incompatible with the intertextual and historical-cultural reading of the Bible. Taken together, they offer both an exegetical starting point for reading the Bible on technology and a warning on appropriate hermeneutical approaches to the Bible.

In the next section, we read perspectives rooted in a classical theological focus on humanity's place in the world, starting from a Patristic-monastic perspective, through Augustinianism and Thomism. In the first essay of this section, P. Hans Sun examines the place of technology in relation to theology as *talk with God* or *talk about God*, rooted in monastic and Patristic writings. Sun notes that the task of theology as *talk with God*, emerging from the asceticism of the Desert Fathers, demands from us that we remove ourselves from the distractions that technologies bring with them in order to experience the stillness of God. Ernest Fortin then reflects on the nature of *ars* in Augustine's writings. Augustine does not embrace a "techno-optimist" position, according to Fortin, but neither does he think technology is evil. Rather, the good works that technology can bring about must be understood as entirely subservient to the good God brings. Following this, Paul Durbin examines the role of modern technologies in the framework of Thomistic natural law. Following the interpretation of natural law propounded by John Courtney Murray and mid-twentieth-century Popes, Durbin suggests a socially-oriented natural law can elucidate and complement many approaches to modern social problems created by new technologies. Willis Dulap's piece concluding this section is not a completed essay, but rather two "fragments" reflecting on the meaning of "natural law" in Christian and Greek frameworks, and considering the ways new technological understandings challenge our understanding of the "natural law."

In the penultimate section of this volume, the question about the modern technological temper is examined from critical theological worldviews. The essays of this section challenge Christians to think of their place in a technological world in a new way. George Grant's essay takes up the difficulty of being genuinely oriented toward *justice*, and the way that technology forecloses our contemplation of this question. Douglas John Hall, who explicitly and positively references Grant's thought, goes further and challenges the North American tendency of theology to provide clear answers instead of authentically engaging the darkness of the world. Thomas Berry poses the difficult challenge of how cosmological stories shape our understanding of our place in the universe. Moderns are caught, Berry supposes, between an outdated, dysfunctional theistic cosmology and an unsatisfactory, demythologized scientific cosmology. To this, he recommends a "New Story" that focuses on differentiation, interior consciousness, and communion with the universe as a whole. Such a vision resonates with George Shields, who outlines a process theology of technology. Such a theology recognizes the inadequacy of science and technology alone to satisfy human desires, but integrates them as part of the human and divine goal toward "satisfactory experience." Finally, Frederick Sontag questions whether the technological vision of human beings as all-powerful is really a good metaphor for God. In this vision, Sontag notes, the problem of theodicy is clearest because we expect God to actively interfere in human activity. Thus, in contrast to Teilhard, Sontag questions the idea of progress and its nihilistic bend in a world still beset by numerous physical and moral evils.

This work concludes with an essay that summarizes and goes beyond the preceding essays. Albert Borgmann evaluates the attitudes and positions articulated by scholars across the two volumes, including Tekippe, Sun, Fortin, Dulap, Durbin, Berry and Shields. While Borgmann notes how they articulate important aspects of the current moment, he expresses dissatisfaction in the ways many reify technological solutions to theological problems. Borgmann focuses on the *quotidianity* of the technological—the way that it absorbs and transforms the "dailiness" of human life. To overcome the consumeristic destining technology sets us up for, he commends the approach of Sun, to find moments of "deliberate and regular counter-practice" wherein we can encounter God.

Before turning to the original essays of this work, I wish to express my deep gratitude to Carl Mitcham for his support and mentorship in this project. I first met Carl in 2017 at the Society for Philosophy and Technology biannual conference in Darmstadt, Germany. I presented a light version of my essay at the end of Volume I, engaging with a thirty-three-year-old text that few else at the conference had heard of, let alone read. To my surprise and joy, he not only attended my talk but also expressed gratitude and constructive criticism to my own response to his work. In the five years since that conference, we have had many fruitful and enriching conversations, both by phone and in person. Carl was the first to suggest to me that I should look for work beyond the borders of the United States, a recommendation I had not seriously considered until then, and so my migration to Hong Kong, as well as my own orientation to Chinese culture and philosophy, owes much to him as well. It is with great pleasure that I offer these essays to the reader and with great pride that I do so with Carl's full support.

Bibliography

Anderson, William H. U., ed. *Theology and Technology*. Wilmington, DE: Vernon Press, 2021.

Barbour, Ian G. *Ethics in an Age of Technology*. The Gifford Lectures 1989–1991 Volume 2. San Francisco: Harper San Francisco, 1993.

Brazal, Agnes, and Kochurani Abraham, eds. *Feminist Cyberethics in Asia: Religious Discourses on Human Connectivity*. New York: Palgrave MacMillan, 2014.

Butler, Philip. *Black Transhuman Liberation Theology: Technology and Spirituality*. London: Bloomsbury, 2019.

Faramelli, Norman J. *Technethics: Christian Mission in an Age of Technology*. New York: Friendship Press, 1971.

Gustafson, James M. "Christian Attitudes toward a Technological Society." *Theology Today* 16, no. 2 (July 1959) 173–187.

Heidegger, Martin. "Hölderlin and the Essence of Poetry." In *The Heidegger Reader*, edited by Günter Figal, translated by Jerome Veith, 117–129. Bloomington: Indiana University Press, 2007.

Jonas, Hans. "Change and Permanence: On the Possibility of Understanding History." In *Philosophical Essays: From Ancient Creed to Modern Man*, 240–263. New York: Atropos Press, 2010.

Tillich, Paul. *The Spiritual Situation in Our Technical Society*. Macon, GA: Mercer University Press, 1988.

Preface (1984)

CARL MITCHAM
JIM GROTE

THIS VOLUME CONTINUES an intellectual assessment of technology that began with Carl Mitcham and Robert Mackey's *Philosophy of Technology: Readings in the Philosophical Problems of Technology* (New York: Free Press, 1972) and has been extended into a number of bibliographies and various general studies. More immediately, it is the outgrowth of a symposium on "Philosophy, Technology and Theology" organized by Mitcham and Grote for the Society of Philosophy and Technology, and held in conjunction with the American Catholic Philosophical Association annual meeting in Toronto, April 20–22, 1979. Initial versions of the papers by Durbin, Fortin, Sun, Schuurman, and Sontag were prepared for this symposium—although Sontag's was not actually delivered there. The paper by George Blair was contributed to a subsequent discussion of the thought of André Malet held under the auspices of the East Central Division of the ACPA in November, 1980, at the Josephinum in Columbus, Ohio. It was while editing these papers for publication in *Research in Philosophy and Technology* that Grote first made the suggestion—about which he has since expressed some misgivings, given the work it has caused him—that they be used as the nucleus for the present book.

Because of its heritage, this collection is somewhat different in character than its philosophical predecessor, which in fact included a section of "Religious Critiques." The present volume assumes the existence of that more "classical" set of texts. It seeks, with judicious selection from a literature of otherwise limited access, complemented by original work, to make a specific argument which is stated at some length in the first essays of each volume. Briefly put, this is that the central question, even in the philosophy of technology, is ultimately theological in character. Whereas the original anthology had tolerantly included religious issues within the scope of technology as a philosophical problem, the present collection wishes to turn the tables and present philosophical issues as the outgrowth of theological understandings. But here it is perhaps appropriate to indicate something of the personal circumstances behind such an idea.

In the Preface to *Philosophy and Technology*, Mitcham and Mackey alluded to a personal philosophical commitment at the basis of their collection which, in religious form, is at the foundation of the present collection as well. The original philosophical commitment was that which in fact makes philosophy possible—that is to the primacy of theory over practice. In truth, because of its character, it is inaccurate to describe it as a commitment; it is a conviction born of reason, but held tenuously in the face of a world manifestly oriented in other directions. Religiously, this becomes a conviction of the primacy of the contemplative life over the active apostolate. In 1967, when the first book was being conceived, Mitcham was neither Catholic nor Christian, and he and Grote were unacquainted. In the early 1970s, Grote, through his involvement with the Catholic Worker movement, developed his own appreciation of the importance of the contemplative dimension of experience. The two became friends through providence as members for a time of a small experimental community near the Abbey of Gethsemani which sought to adapt the Western contemplative monastic tradition to family life. This work is thus part of an on-going pilgrimage to integrate the intellectual and spiritual dimensions of our lives. The ghost of Thomas Merton hovers over, without necessarily approving of, such efforts.

Essay 1

Technology as a Theological Problem in the Christian Tradition

Carl Mitcham

Technology is currently recognized as a social and as a philosophical problem—but only to some limited extent as a properly theological one. Theology has generally concentrated on analyzing an apparently contingent or disconnected series of moral problems obviously engendered by technology (industrial alienation, nuclear weapons, the social justice of development, biomedical engineering, mass media, etc.) without either systematically relating such specific issues or grounding them in more fundamental reflections on the relationship between Christian faith and technological reason.

The present collection of original essays and translations proposes to initiate a comprehensive theological reflection in two ways: by indicating the basic issues of faith and reason as they are manifested anew in the interaction between Christianity and technology and by exploring themes which emerge in the theological reassessment of the Christian heritage from the perspective engendered by modern technological development.

The limitation of this analysis to the Christian tradition can be explained on two grounds. Practically speaking, some restrictions simply have to be made. The subject of the relationship between religion as a whole and technology in general is just too broad, and too nebulous, to be fruitfully pursued at the present stage of theological discourse. Theoretically speaking, it seems reasonable to focus on the confrontation between Christianity and modern technology because of the close historical association between the two—an association which must not, however, be taken to speak for itself. The historical engagement between Christianity and technology is itself a question for theological analysis, in order to try to determine its essential and accidental features. Furthermore, it is by means of the prosecution of theological reflections on technology within specific religious traditions that more ecumenical reflection will eventually be made possible.

1.

The question of the relationship between Christianity and technology sounds conspicuously like a number of other questions. What is the relationship between Christianity and art? Christianity and science? Christianity and philosophy? Christianity and politics? Is there such a thing as a Christian art or science or philosophy or politics?

Such questions have generally been subject to two inadequate kinds of answers. The first is to reply that, Yes, there is a Christian art. This art is identified with one whose subject matter is overtly Christian. The second is to reply that, No, there is not some specifically Christian art. There is only a Christian attitude toward art.

The weakness of the first answer is exposed by the rich history of Christian art, which exhibits an enormous diversity in style; and by the fact that many devout artists have dealt with Christian themes in quite subtle, indirect, or allusive ways. Christian themes often shade imperceptibly into general human themes. Indeed, this is exactly what one would expect, if one believes that Christianity is a true response to certain fundamental aspects of the human condition.

In light of such considerations, the second answer has usually been formulated. Its weakness, however, is that it often leaves the issue in a rather nebulous state. If there is a truly Christian attitude toward art, what is it? The truth is that in different historical periods Christians have taken quite different attitudes toward art, and science, and philosophy, and politics. Even in the same historical period, equally orthodox Christians have argued quite different attitudes toward each or all of these aspects of culture. While the first answer provides a very specific answer that is unable to encompass a wealth of relevant examples, the second is able to encompass all possible examples only at the expense of becoming virtually vacuous.

In what has become a classic of American theology, H. Richard Niebuhr's *Christ and Culture* (1951) offers a detailed articulation of the second kind of answer, by examining five different forms of the Christian attitude toward art, science, politics, and economics. Given the fact that our culture is now widely recognized to be predominantly technological in character, one can expect the alternative formulations in question to be reproduced in Christian attitudes toward modern technology.

According to Niebuhr, who admits to building upon the work of Ernst Troelstch in his analysis, the five basic relationships between Christ and culture are as follows: (1) Christ and culture in opposition; (2) Christ and culture in fundamental agreement; (3) Christ above culture; (4) Christ and culture in paradox; and (5) Christ the transformer of culture. The essays in Volume I exhibit in turn these same five relationships between Christ and modern technology.

George Blair, in "Faith Outside Technique," argues that faith is an attitude or *theoria* or acceptance which is fundamentally opposed to all *praxis*, particularly the pursuit of technological control or domination. Indeed, for Blair faith is even opposed to all teleological *theoria*, that is natural science, whether in Aristotelian or modern form. Faith simply does not look at the world in terms of its processes and relations, purposes and uses. The world can, of course, be so approached—and manipulated as a result. But such is not the choice of true faith.

In this argument Blair can be allied with previous Christian criticisms of the "world," Greco-Roman and nineteenth-century bourgeois culture, not to mention modern industrial technology—as illustrated by the teachings of the first letter of John, Tertullian, Kierkegaard, and Leo Tolstoy, respectively. But he exhibits even closer affinities to the Christian mystical tradition. This can be seen by comparing Blair's ideas with Meister Eckhart's argument for detachment and his disciple Angelus Silesius's saying that "the rose is without why." The mystical tradition has in fact been developed into an implicit criticism of modern technology by some of its contemporary followers.

Consider, for instance, Thomas Merton's meditation on "Rain and the Rhinoceros," in which he rejects the rhinoceros-like idea that everything must have some use or purpose. "The universal and modern man is the man . . . who cannot understand that a *living thing might perhaps be without usefulness*; nor does he understand that, at bottom, it is the useful that may be a useless . . . burden," writes Merton, quoting a complaint by Eugene Ionesco on the New York production of his play, *Rhinoceros*, as a farce. In contrast Merton appeals to the "gratuity" and "meaninglessness" of the rain, "because it reminds me again and again that the whole world runs by rhythms I have not yet learned to recognize, rhythms that are not those of the engineer." And to those who try to give some utility or purpose in his own monastic vocation, by viewing the monastery as a power-house of prayer or some other absurdity, Merton asks, "Can't I just be in the woods without any special reason? Just being in the woods, at night, in the cabin, is something too excellent to be justified or explained! It just is."[1] In faith, too, Blair argues, we approach the world simply for what it is, with zen-like acceptance.

The exact opposite position is taken by Wilhelm Fudpucker, who, in "Through Christian Technology to Technological Christianity," argues the essential unity of Christian practice and modern technology, thus allying himself with the long tradition of culture-Christianity. Attempts to identify Christianity and some prevailing culture extend from the gnostics and Constantine (on the levels of theory and practice, respectively) to the Enlightenment interpretations of John Locke (*The Reasonableness of Christianity*, 1695), Immanuel Kant (*Religion within the Bounds of Reason Alone*, 1793), and Friedrich Schleiermacher (*Lectures on Religion to Its Cultural Despisers*, 1799). Schleiermacher, for instance, was, in Niebuhr's words, "determined to be both a Christo-centric theologian and a modern man, participating fully in the work of culture."[2] This led him, when defending Christianity against its cultured intellectual critics, to interpret the Christian religion in terms of its contributions to culture, and culture in terms of its compatibility with Christianity. Fudpucker's argument for the intimate historical and sociological harmony between the demands of Christianity and those of technology, interpreting each in terms of the other, fits squarely into this tradition.

Niebuhr makes one observation on the opposition versus unification debate that throws a special light on the Christ-against-technology versus the Christ-of-technology version of this debate. Behind all Christ-of-culture theologies lies the usually unstated thesis that the human situation is fundamentally characterized by a conflict between man (and his culture) against nature. In this situation, Christianity readily sides with the human. Christ-against-culture theology, by contrast, is based on the romantic premise of a fundamental conflict between the truly human

1. Merton, *Raids on the Unspeakable*, 13. Previous quotations come from pages 21 and 9, respectively.

2. Niebuhr, *Christ and Culture*, 93.

and the artificialities of culture. In this case, of course, Christianity just as readily sides with man and is opposed to culture. Since technology is in some obvious sense a conquest of nature, it is thus to be expected that any Christian theology which takes the fundamental hiatus of the human condition as one between the human and the natural will also tend to identify Christ with technology.

Blair and Fudpucker represent polar opposite positions. The next three theologies of the Christ-technology relationship are variations of an intermediate position. This intermediate position takes the fundamental conflict in reality as being neither between Christian man and culture nor between man and nature, but between man and God. Contra the Christ-against-culture position, the three intermediate views argue that human beings are invariably and necessarily part of some culture. Contra the Christ-of-culture position, they argue that culture is based upon and perfects nature. Culture, and hence technology, is sometimes on one side, sometimes on the other of the man/God hiatus. The line of division has to be drawn not to one side or the other of culture, but through it.

According to Niebuhr's analysis of the first of these three intermediate positions, that of Christ above culture, what distinguishes it is a recognition of true culture as a positive achievement in itself, but one which is also preparatory to supernatural synthesis with Christ. Christ and culture are really distinct but can be synthesized at a supernatural level. Historical culture is a preparation for transhistorical union with God. Grace builds not only on nature, but on the perfection of nature in culture. This is a position represented classically by Clement of Alexandria and St. Thomas Aquinas.

Terry Tikeppe's "Bernard Lonergan: A Context for Technology," shows how the transcendental Thomism of Lonergan gives this approach a typically modern twist. In accordance with the Kantian revolution in philosophy, Lonergan shifts the focus from transcendence to immanence and analyzes the ways in which the conundrums of technological practice require a supernatural synthesis without, however, affirming the positive existencc of a transcendent or supernatural reality. In itself technology contains elements of both progress and decline. A technical solution to some human problem applies and proliferates practical insight. In response to the need for transportation comes the invention of cars. The widespread use of cars creates urban congestion, which gives rise to proposals for large-scale transportation networks. The optimistic conclusion is a vision of increasingly powerful technological fixes to human problems.

But side by side with progressive insight and successful action comes increasing oversight and technological failure. The unintended side-effects of technical solutions often outpace man's technological genius. Cars give rise to pollution; transportation networks break down under slighted maintenance, labor demands, and shifting patterns of economic development. Human intelligence, especially in its practical forms, is limited by immediate utilitarian prejudice as much as it is oriented toward the truth. Man is always overlooking some aspect of things; he fails to take in the whole picture. Because of this coordination of progress and decline, the realm of humanly distressing disorder gradually shifts from the natural to the technological milieu. Today it is environmental pollution and nuclear weapons which threaten human life more than plagues or bad weather. But this technological disorder and danger can only be overcome by union with faith, in which God communicates to human beings a higher vision and thus collaborates with them in transcending their technological limitations.

For André Malet, representing what Niebuhr calls a dualist approach, the realms of technology and faith remain unalterably separate—not opposed, but separate. "The Believer in the Presence of Technology" uses Heidegger's analysis of technology to provide a description of the world in the new or modern sense of that term, and then asks how the man of faith should respond to that reality. Following St. Paul and Martin Luther, Malet argues that the believer must at once acknowledge the value of this world and keep it distinct from faith. The real problem is the contamination of one by the other.

The tensions of this coexistence are paradoxical. Unlike a Christ-above-technology theology, the acknowledgement of technological achievement is done almost exclusively in negative terms. Technology is more a hedge against disaster than a positive achievement. It wars against plague and famine, more than it constructs civilization. In itself it can be said to be representative more of the wrath of God than of his mercy. But the believer must accept the fact that for the present he is inextricably involved with this world and must therefore participate in it on its own terms. Malet relates Christ and technology after the manner of Luther's argument for the simultaneous practice of love (see *On Christian Liberty*, 1520) and vengeance (see *Against the Robbing and Murdering Hordes of Peasants*, 1525). To quote Luther's defense of his dual counsel, "There are two kingdoms, one the kingdom of God, the other the kingdom of the world . . . .God's kingdom is a kingdom of grace and mercy . . . but the kingdom of the world is a kingdom of wrath and severity . . . .Now he who would confuse these two . . . would put wrath into God's kingdom and mercy into the world's kingdom, and that is the same as putting the devil in heaven and God in hell."[3]

The typical Protestant emphasis on a separation between church and state is extended by Malet into a call for the proper separation between "the scientific-technical project and the project of faith." Technology, like politics, is a problem only when it infects faith or is infected by it. Grace and nature are both served by a proper recognition of their dual functions.

But does such a separation not call into question God's love for the world and the power of grace? Contra Malet, Egbert Schuurman, in "Technology in a Christian-Theological Perspective," takes what Niebuhr calls a conversionist position. Grace is able to enter into and transform nature, or that already once-transformed nature called culture, or in the present instance technology—without necessarily being contaminated by it. This is an idea which is expressed in different forms by the Gospel of John, St. Augustine, John Wesley, and Frederick Denison Maurice insofar as each presents Christ as able to alter or change the world. In the case of Saints John and Augustine the world in question is classical pagan culture; for Wesley and Maurice there is explicit reference to the world of industrial technology. Indeed, the same issue is one of John Calvin's arguments with Luther, and the reason why Calvin was willing to establish a church city-state at Geneva.

With Schuurman, the issue is made more tractable by arguing that the essential problem with modern technology is the motive behind it. Motives (and ideas) are more amenable to Christian conversion than practices and institutions, which often tend to exhibit long term resistance to transformative change even when they appear short term docile participants. Besides, according to Schuurman, a mandate for cultural work was given to man by God from the very beginning. Although corrupted by man's sinful pursuit of power, it can be redeemed, even in its technological manifestation, through Christ. The conversionist, as Niebuhr points out, tends to understand history, at least since Christ, as an on-going story of God's mighty deeds and the human response.

3. Luther, "An Open Letter on the Harsh Book Against the Peasants," 69–70. Quoted also by Niebuhr, *Christ and Culture*, 171–172.

The conversionist "lives somewhat less 'between the times' of Christ's first and second coming and somewhat more in the divine 'now' than do his brother Christians."[4] With Schuurman, too, now is the time for man to respond in faith to the challenge of technology, to turn from bad to good motives and thus transform his technological practice. Thus, as Niebuhr says with reference to St. Augustine, technology may become both the beneficiary of the conversion of man's love and the instrument "of that new love of God that rejoices in His whole creation and serves all His creatures."[5]

In making his argument, Schuurman points up better than either Tekippe or Malet some of the theological doctrines upon which all three intermediate positions of synthesis, dualism, and conversion are founded. Contra the Christ-of-technology position, centerists stress the real distinction between Christ and at least the present form of technology. Yet granted that God is the original creator of the world and/or nature, Christ as God cannot be completely opposed to it. At some deep level, all creation desires to be obedient to God. As a result of sin and the fall, however, man cannot do this on his own. He must rely on grace, especially as manifested in the salvation of Jesus Christ. The primacy of grace overshadows the greatness of all works, no matter how good.

2.

The appeal to such theological principles can be taken to shift the point of discussion away from an articulation of formal alternatives and toward substantive issues of truth or orthodoxy. Which position is based on the more orthodox foundations? Which accurately utilizes those doctrines which are most appropriate to the interpretation of modern technology? Niebuhr evidently leans toward one of the centerist positions by indicating his belief that according to the Bible the basic conflict is between man and God, not between man and culture or nature. It appears likely that he also leans more toward the conversionist than any other of the centerist positions, although he effects a studied neutrality among the three, carefully considering the theological strengths and weaknesses of each.

Niebuhr likewise avoids any attempt at a "scientific conclusion" which would reconcile the various positions in some comprehensive

4. Niebuhr, *Christ and Cutlure* 195.

5. Niebuhr, *Christ and Culture*, 215.

general theory. His conclusion is that to try to give "the Christian answer" to the Christ-culture problem "would be an act of usurpation of the Lordship of Christ;" although given the demands of life, each believer must make his own decision between the various alternatives. There is a strong implication that sometimes one choice will be more historically appropriate than another. And Niebuhr explicitly maintains that to study the alternatives is itself an encounter with how Christ has manifested himself in the past which can enter into a responsible, personal decision for the present. This is what he calls "social existentialism," or individual response to Christ arising out of a lived contact with the historical and social community of the Christian tradition.

In emphasizing choice alone, however, Niebuhr comes close to a kind of voluntarism that would make freedom an empty act. And by shying away from any substantive argument about which alternative is in truth appropriate to the present historical situation, he bypasses an opportunity to witness to the fullness of his own encounter with Christ. It is with such considerations in mind that we undertake to argue for the first and fourth alternative theologies of the Christ-technology relationship as being the most adequate for our time—although not necessarily in the formulations provided by Blair and Malet.

Blair's downgrading of charity and Malet's use of Heidegger are both problematic. Blair clearly leaves out a whole dimension of the Christian experience. And contrary to Malet, the "groaning of nature" may well be for release from domination by a fallen human technology. But by emphasizing the difference between Christ and technology, Blair and Malet nevertheless throw necessary and clarifying light on an issue otherwise highly clouded by naivete, sentiment, and self-interest. An argument to this effect will be made in three steps: first, by noting some weaknesses of the Christ-of-technology, Christ-above-technology, and Christ-the-transformer-of-technology positions; second, by considering a way in which Niebuhr has failed to do full justice to the Christ-against-culture position; and third, by specifying the strengths of a modified oppositionist/dualist position in the setting of a highly technological culture.

The weaknesses of Fudpucker, Tekippe-Lonergan, and Schuurman can be read as permutations of politico-religious idealism. Each fails in special ways to recognize what is really going on with technology, and as a result lets mere good intentions or wishes play too strong a role in the formation of their attitudes. Of these, Fudpucker is no doubt the most outrageous, although he expresses a point of view which is not easily dismissed. The widespread popularity of his mentor Teilhard de Chardin is witness to this. Yet the hypothesis of Christianity as the historical basis of modern technology rests on no more than the existential tautology that a worldly Christianity has worldly effects. It does not examine the orthodoxy of such a worldly Christianity, which Niebuhr rightly shows to be lacking. It likewise exhibits marked similarities to that conservative reaction to the French Revolution which would make Christianity the foundation of all social order—a dubious justification, to say the least. And the fact that contemporary technology may well make heroic Christian virtue a categorical necessity in no way proves that such virtue is any more likely to be practiced now than it ever has been in the past. The myth of a secular Christianity, to which even Jacques Maritain appeals in his pompous speculations on a "new Christendom,"[6] is undercut by the simple fact that modern technology raises grave impediments to any normal Christian way of life. Finally, Fudpucker's spirituality of historic progress reveals a heritage of heretical millennial speculations.

Tekippe-Lonergan has the virtue of highlighting precisely what Fudpucker ignores, that is, the Janus-faced character of technological progress that rests on certain inherent limitations to this expansion of moral virtue. There are a number of interesting parallel sociological formulations of Lonergan's insight. Karl Marx's analysis of a conflict between techno-economic base and politico-cultural superstructure is one case in point; William F. Ogburn' s concept of a "cultural lag" between social and technical development is another; Alvin Toffler's idea of "future shock" is still another. But it was actually Maritain, the leading neo-Thomist of a prior generation, who originally formulated Lonergan's principle.

On a number of occasions Maritain describes what he terms "the double movement of history." For instance, in commenting on the parable of the weeds in the field of wheat (Matthew 13:24–30) Maritain concludes that both good and evil are permanent aspects of the human condition, and that both are simply amplified by technological development.[7] Yet neither Maritain nor Lonergan seems able to recognize the

6. Maritain, *Integral Humanism*. This is the second translation of *Humanisme Integral*, first published in 1936. See, e.g., page 123: "We are thus justified in thinking that the growth in awareness of the temporal office of the Christian calls for a new style of sanctity, which one can characterize above all as the sanctity and sanctification of secular life."

7. Jacques Maritain so often recycles not just thoughts (we all do that) but whole verbatim paragraphs, that it is difficult to know from where to cite. The most extensive presentation of his "Axiomatic Formulas or Functional Laws" of history occurs in *On*

obvious implication, that the simultaneous increase of both good and bad effects becomes at some point in itself evil.[8] The best that Lonergan can do is to argue that the coordination of progress and decline demands a solution or intervention from on high. The possibility that this need might not be met is, however, left up in the air. Like Heidegger, Lonergan winds up waiting on unnamed gods.

---

the Philosophy of History, chapter 2. But see also *Integral Humanism,*108ff; *The Rights of Man and Natural Law,* 29–30; and *Theonas,* 113. A quotation from this last-named source: "Though the law of progress tends to dominate in history whenever the effort of the mind is able to succeed—especially in the order of individual technique—yet the law of human beings is the most part not of progress, but of alternation—the law of generation and corruption. There is one human thing, it is true, that is an exception—the Church, which must grow and be made perfect to the fullness of the age of Christ, and which will know no decline. But that is precisely because it is not only human but divine." Plus another from a footnote on page 111 of *Integral Humanism*: "Because of the weakness of our species, evil is more frequent than good among men; and in the growth of history, it grows and deepens at the same time as the good mingled with it . . . . Yet if evil is a permanent feature of the human condition, then it behooves human beings either to limit the destructive powers at their command or to admit that it may be the will of God for the human race to destroy itself." Maritain, however, maintains that "genuine Christianity . . . abhors the pessimism of inertia." *On the Philosophy of History,* 50.

8. An argument to this effect has been made by Lyons, "Are Luddites Confused?" 381–403. One difficulty with the argument, however, is that it must ultimately confront what Hannah Arendt correctly terms the "banality of evil" and the corresponding secrecy of the good. An aspect of this is that it often appears that the good side of technological development is primarily actual (health and wealth), whereas the bad side remains mostly a mere possibility (i.e., nuclear war). But true goods are more obscure (virtue and wisdom), and given a long enough time all possibilities will become actual. At least this is a principle of Thomistic metaphysics (see St. Thomas Aquinas's "third way"). Once nuclear war becomes actual, previous technological development cannot help but take on a very different character- the same way a speeding joyride in a car comes to be looked at very differently by those involved after it leads to a bad wreck. The problem of terrorism and technology needs to be seriously considered at this point as well, and never is.

Another aspect of this issue: Although a 10% chance that some technology might cause one hundred deaths (e.g., a Roman bridge collapse) and a .001 % chance that something else might cause one million deaths (nuclear reactor meltdown) mathematically create the same risk factor, the second presents a far greater biological threat. It is a lot easier for a species and environment to adjust to a hundred deaths every now and then than for it to absorb one million deaths all at once. Needless to add, when technology starts running the chance of wiping out the whole human race, even if that chance remains infinitesimally small, it presents a much more serious biological threat than the regular death of 50% of the children under the age of six, which poses no biological threat to the species at all.

Schuurman at least names the god and proposes a way to get him involved in dealing with the problems at hand. Jesus Christ is the answer to the destructive impulses of progress, and he can come into play in the historical world by means of individual conversion. Schuurman's approach is almost necessarily the approach of all preaching. Certainly, such diverse persons as Baptist evangelicals and Pope John Paul II have also used this approach. Indeed, a conversionist theology may be at the heart of that oft-remarked association between fundamentalism and worldly power, whether it be found in Billy Graham or the Roman Curia. For a conversionist it is adequate to "love and do what you will." Good intentions are what is essential.

The problem with good intentions, though, is that they are not necessarily intelligent about their own application and consequences, nor are they self-reinforcing. The incarnation of good intentions is no easier to effect in the world than it is in oneself. And in the modern world the revivalist spirit, naively trusting to itself, winds up subjecting itself to a continuous string of temptations which only the heroically virtuous will overcome. Even the great preacher John Wesley realized that conversion often produces a frugality and discipline which in turn engenders riches which then undermine the original conversion.[9] For most of the converted it will be necessary to construct an artificial environment to support and strengthen the initial conversion experience.

Consider, for instance, a short case history illustrating both the strengths and weaknesses of Schuurman's Christ-as-transformer-of-technology position, but from a somewhat oblique perspective. In northern California there used to be a small intentional community which practiced a Zen Buddhist spiritual discipline. Houses and environment were carefully constructed and maintained to reflect and promote an attitude of what in Buddhism is called mindfulness. The place displayed an austere physical simplicity not unlike a Shaker village, and its members had an aura of intenseness that sometimes put visitors off. At some point, however, the whole group converted to a fundamentalist version of Christianity. The particulars surrounding this are not important to present purposes. As a result they came to believe that the attention they gave

9. "Does it not seem . . . that Christianity . . . has a tendency . . . to undermine and destroy itself? For wherever true Christianity spreads, it must cause diligence and frugality, which, in the natural course of things, must beget riches! and riches naturally beget pride, love of the world, and every temper that is destructive of Christianity." Wesley, Sermon CXVI, 290.

to the material details of life constituted a kind of worldliness, even idolatry. And so their environment slowly but surely became prey to television sets, plastic dishes, and precooked food. Austere simplicity was replaced by a joyful clutter and a diminution of intensity that eventually led to the disbanding of the group.[10]

This example leads into the second stage of the argument for a modified oppositionist/dualist position—the fact that Niebuhr has not done the Christ-against-culture theology full justice. He does not recognize that in most cases the opposition in question is not against culture in general, but only against some specific culture. The author of 1 John rejects the "world" but counsels obedience to the new law and commandments. Likewise for Tertullian, for St. Benedict, and even for Tolstoy, it is a particular form of godless culture that is rejected—in the name of an attempt to establish a more god-filled or god-reflecting culture. At the same time, it is almost never assumed, contrary to what Niebuhr intimates, that the new culture can be identified in any simple way with Christ. There is no flip-flop from Christ-against-culture into Christ-of-culture theology.

Niebuhr's strongest but undeveloped example of the Christ-against-culture theology, that is monasticism, best illustrates this point. The Rule of St. Benedict is quite critical of secular culture, but in no way rejects culture *in toto*. In fact, it seeks to articulate a different kind of culture, which is why it spends so much time spelling out the details of things like how to recite the psalms, do spiritual reading, handle tools, etc. There is a rejection of one set of technical activities (those ordered toward gaining honor and power or making money) in favor of another set of technical activities (saying the psalms and spiritual reading). Nevertheless, this new set of techniques in no way becomes identified with that purity of heart which is the ultimate goal of the monastic ascesis. It is clearly relegated to the position of a subordinate means.

The monastery is compared to a school. It is a structured environment which attempts to exclude some activities and to make others more likely to occur. But it recognizes that the occurrence of these other activities remains ultimately problematic. Indeed, as all teachers know, this is true with regard to learning in a secular context as well. Teachers need the structure of tests and grades to encourage students to learn, but they do not make the mistake of identifying learning with getting good

10. For some discussion of the need for Christian community see Berger, *A Rumor of Angels*, chapter 1, "The Alleged Demise," and Berger, *The Sacred Canopy*, chapter 6, "Secularization and the Problem of Plausibility?"

grades. Only those outside a school or monastery make the simplistic mistake of identifying the culture in question and its end or purpose. Only someone outside a monastery could think that being a monk in itself makes a person holy. Monks themselves know better and make a significant effort to disabuse newcomers and outsiders (and themselves) of such illusions. Indeed, such a disillusioning technique forms part of the structure of a well-ordered monastery.

With the recognition of this weakness in Niebuhr's analysis of the Christ-against-culture theology, the oppositionist and dualist positions begin to exhibit certain important similarities. Oppositionist theology can in fact contribute a necessary correction for that tendency in dualism which would grant too great an autonomy to the realm of secular culture or technique. But to broach this issue leads to the third stage of the argument, a consideration of the strengths of a modified oppositionist/dualist theology of technology.

The strengths of an oppositionist/dualist theology can be summarized as three-fold: It is in harmony with the fundamental aspect of religious experience in general. It represents a sound generalization of the Christian theology of sacred technique. And it clarifies that intuitive Christian reaction to secular technique manifested in opposition to certain specific forms of technology (money, nuclear weapons, abortion, etc.).

According to Mircea Eliade and other historians of religion, the fundamental religious experience is that of some sacred reality (whether object or event) which is different or other than the secular or everyday reality in its revelatory or hierophantic character. "The first possible definition of the *sacred* is that it is *the opposite of the profane*."[11] Moses standing before the burning bush recognized it as different from all other bushes in the desert. The exodus from Egypt is an event unlike all others in its power to reveal the relationship between the Lord and his people Israel. For the Christian, Jesus Christ is the unique God-man, and the eucharist is a meal unlike all others. For the Muslim, the Kaaba is not just another rock; it is a stone from heaven. The oppositionist theology recognizes technology as the contemporary form of the profane and thus presents Christ as something wholly other than this profane reality.

But the sacred is at once other than and the same as the profane. It is "the manifestation of something of a wholly different order, a reality that

11. Eliade, *The Sacred and the Profane*, 10.

does not belong to our world, in objects that are an integral part of our natural 'profane' world." "By manifesting the sacred, any object becomes *something else*, yet it continues to remain *itself*" as well."[12] The exodus is not just an event of salvation history, it is also an event of history. The eucharist remains bread and wine at the same time that it becomes the body and blood of Jesus Christ. The Kaaba is not just a stone from heaven, it is a rock on this earth in the city of Mecca. In like manner, that which is wholly other than technique is also a kind of technique. For the Christian the paradigm of sacred technique can be found in the eucharist and the other sacraments.

The orthodox Christian theology of sacred technique is one of paradoxical dualism. On the one hand, the eucharist is to be repeated in the ritual manner exactly as Jesus Christ instructed his disciples. It has an objective or formal character, the technical completion of which constitutes it as a sacred reality or vehicle of grace. On the other hand, there is no identification of the sacred ritual with sacredness itself. It is merely an "outward and visible sign of an inward and invisible grace," as the traditional catechism has it. The reception of such grace remains problematic and dependent on our own inward and invisible faith. A clear sign against any magical identification of the sacred technique with holiness itself is the presence of Judas Iscariot, who betrayed the Lord, at its very institution. Judas partook of the sacred meal but did not become a saint.

The dualist attitude toward technology in general (at least as presented by Niebuhr's analysis of Luther) can be read as a generalization of the Christian attitude toward sacred technique and thus in need of qualification. What applies to sacred technique is not necessarily always true of technique in general. On the one hand, Luther affirms secular technologies as independent realities.

> "Music," said Luther, "is a noble gift of God." Commerce was also open to the Christian for "buying and selling are necessary. They cannot be dispensed with and can be practiced in a Christian manner." Political activities, and even the career of the soldier, were even more necessary to the common life, and were therefore spheres in which the neighbor could be served and God be obeyed . . . .In all these vocations, in all this cultural work in the service of others, the technical rules of that particular work needed to be followed. A Christian was not only free to work in culture but free to choose those methods which were called for

12. Eliade, *The Sacred and the Profane*, 12.

> . . . .As he cannot derive the laws of medical procedure from the gospel when he deals with a case of typhus, so he cannot deduce from the commandment of love the specific laws to be enacted in a commonwealth containing criminals.[13]

On the other hand, Luther is equally careful to make clear that although a Christian *can* follow Christ in all such secular actions, practicing some secular profession is *not* in itself equivalent to following Christ. As Niebuhr summarizes the point of issue, "No increase of scientific and technical knowledge can renew the spirit within us."[14]

There is, then, a distinction between the how of technique and the spiritual purpose for which that technique might be practiced. Yet it is this second moment of the dualist dialectic that most often gets overlooked in what Max Weber referred to as "the Protestant ethic"—partly because Luther was so struck by and willing to grant to secular technologies the abstract possibility of being pursued within a Christian spirit. In a highly technological and secular culture, however, it becomes necessary to re-emphasize the limitations to such a possibility, perhaps most directly by making use of an oppositionist theology of technology. Although all the evidence on secularization is not in, it is at least reasonable to argue that it may intensify faith in the few. St. Paul's observation that "where sin increased, grace abounded all the more" (Romans 5:20) is in no way intended as a guide for action, as St. Paul himself indicates (Romans 6:1–2). Besides, as Aristotle notes in a different but related context, although the life of virtue is not to be identified with the life of restraint, still in most cases even for the few the life of restraint is closer to the life of virtue than is the life of pleasure.[15]

The truth is, though, that even Luther excluded some techniques from those which could be practiced by the Christian or which the Christian could reasonably be expected to imbue with a Christian spirit. And at some subconscious level many Christians have recognized the realistic wisdom of separating their lives from the insidious influences of certain techniques. The most well-known are the early Christian rejection of bearing arms, the medieval prohibition of usury, and the contemporary arguments against artificial contraception and abortion. But there have

13. Niebuhr, *Christ and Culture*, 174–175.

14. Niebuhr, *Christ and Culture*, 176.

15. See Aristotle, *Nicomachean Ethics*, Book II, 2 (esp. 1104a34–1104b4) and 8-9 (esp. 1109a15–16 and 1109b5–10).

been many other realistic arguments for the delimitation of technology within the Christian tradition—from the iconoclastic debate on holy images to the Puritan concern about certain forms of art and literature and Amish restrictions on mechanization. Indeed, a strong case can be made for associating the most vital periods of Christian life and work precisely with such anti-technological attitudes.

In any case, it is an oppositionist/dualist theology of technology which can best begin to appreciate the issues involved in the intuitive Christian reaction against certain techniques, even though in any one instance a particular version of such a theology might argue for different conclusions. It is also from such an oppositionist/dualist position that the most fruitful exegesis of the tension between technology and the Christian tradition can begin. Indeed, it is just such an attitude which is manifested in the majority of exegetical studies constituting Part II of the present collection.[16]

Bibliography

Berger, Peter L. *A Rumor of Angels*. Garden City, NY: Doubleday Anchor, 1970.

———. *The Sacred Canopy: Elements of a Sociological Theory of Religion*. Garden City, NY: Doubleday Anchor, 1968.

Eliade, Mircea. *The Sacred and the Profane*. New York: Harcourt Brace & World, 1959.

Luther, Martin. *An Open Letter on the Harsh Book Against the Peasants*. Luther's Works 46. Philadelphia: Fortress, 1967.

Lyons, Dan. "Are Luddites Confused?" *Inquiry* 22, No. 4 (Winter 1979) 381–403.

Maritain, Jacques. *Integral Humanism: Temporal and Spiritual Problems of a New Christendom*. Translated by Joseph W. Evans. New York: Scribner, 1968.

———. *On the Philosophy of History*. Edited by Joseph Owens. New York: Scribner, 1957.

———. *The Rights of Man and Natural Law*. Translated by Doris C. Anson. New York: Scribner, 1943.

———. *Theonas*. Translated by F. J. Sheed. New York: Sheed & Ward, 1933.

Merton, Thomas. *Raids on the Unspeakable*. New York: New Directions, 1964.

Niebuhr, H. Richard. *Christ and Culture*. New York: Harper & Row, 1951.

Wesley, John. "Sermon CXVI." In *Works of John Wesley* Vol. VII (Grand Rapids, MI: Zondervan, 1872).

16. Editor's note: The essays of "Part II" are published in volume II of this work.

Essay 2

Faith Outside Technique

George A. Blair

1.

Christianity is something utterly other than technique; it involves a way of looking at things that is foreign to the way in which the technical mentality views things.

Interestingly, it is not teleology that distinguishes the Christian way of thinking from the technical one. Although it has often been argued that Christian theology views the world teleologically, whereas technology does not, in fact technology is itself inherently teleological in its presuppositions. Even though the technician is exerting efficient causality, he is able to *predict* what will happen; and this means he knows the *end* results beforehand. He *thinks* this is due to his efficient causality; but it is more due to the structure of the object he is working on. There is a finality in his materials, which is what really makes it possible for him to predict what will happen. A person must add energy to a mixture of hydrogen and oxygen to get water (so an efficient cause is necessary); but that the result will be water and not table salt is predictable because of the structure of the material, not because of the energy added. Water is produced whether the energy added is heat, electricity, or mechanical energy; water is not produced if the mixture is not hydrogen and oxygen.

In this regard it is important to distinguish technology from technique: as I see it, technology implicitly recognizes a finality in things, and makes predictions based on that finality. Technique is the fallacy that the predictability due solely to the efficient cause, ignoring the finality in the material. The "sin" of technique, if you will, is the sense of omniscience ("*I* was the one who did this"), and the refusal to submit to the reality worked upon. The only time the reality of the material is recognized is when some counter tendencies are set up in it and something unwanted happens.

To focus, as some have done,[1] on "the groaning of nature" as a theological justification for and reconciliation with technology is therefore not necessarily to escape from technique. If one sees nature as groaning, one sees it as in an evil state; and the temptation is to impose upon it what we think the "good" state is, irrespective of the good aspects of its present condition. Does the air "want" to be unpolluted? Is it "groaning" to be so? I doubt it. Can it be cleaned up? Yes, if we do certain things. Should it be cleaned up? It depends. The person who says it is Christian to clean up the air because it is groaning to be cleaned is imposing a finality on the air that simply does not exist. The air is not in imbalance as dirty; it is not "naturally headed toward" cleanness. Air does not, as some ecologists argue, "cleanse itself if we just leave it alone"; the Smokey Mountains testify to this. It cleanses itself sometimes, and it makes itself filthy sometimes-without our ever lifting a finger. He who, in the name of Christianity, cleans up the air is not "helping it to be itself," but is imposing his abstract idea of the way he thinks the world "ought" to be upon a world out of which this idea did not arise. The air is indifferent to being dirty or clean in itself.

The opposition between technique and Christianity does not come from the technological use of the world for our own purposes; that sort of thing can be Christianized quite easily. Technology as such is not anti-Christian. Technique is anti-Christian, however, because it uses the world as if it has no other reality than to do my will—as if it were a pure vehicle for me to achieve my goals. As such, technique is trying to pretend that it is God, who can create out of nothing, which is anti-Christian.

There is also a variant of the technical mentality which infects a good deal of Christian thinking. Technique recognizes no finality in nature itself (and assumes all finalities are put there by man); this variation assumes that it knows what the finality is in nature, and so "cooperates" with nature by making nature go in the "known" or "proper" direction-when in fact this direction is just one of the many directions nature can

1. See, e.g., André Malet's use of Romans 8:19–22 in section 2 of his "The Believer in the Presence of Technique."

go, and is no more "the purpose God had in mind" than any other direction. This is imposing a human finality on nature as if it were either nature's own or God's finality, and others were not "natural" or were "contrary to what God intended."

Why can I say this? Because of what a finality in nature is. As Aristotle himself knew, a natural (as opposed to a chosen) finality is nothing more than a tendency of something in an unstable condition (Aristotle's "being in potency") to achieve a certain definite equilibrium (the "act" that it was "deprived" of by being in potency). This predictable stable condition at the end of a process is, of course, tautologously the end. What has caused trouble is that Aristotle defined "the good" as the end. He did not call the end good; he defined the good as the end. Thus, also tautologously, every change is for the good. But this applies to destructive as well as constructive changes; the mature state is the good of the growing organism, and the decayed corpse is the good of the dying organism.[2]

Now if one takes a different view of the good, so that there are some things that are better than others, and still others that are positively bad, and one superimposes this on Aristotle's analysis, then destructive changes (i.e. ones that human beings look on, from their special viewpoint, as bad) are not the "real" ends that things have, and are somehow "unnatural," because "nature tends toward the good." But the principle that "nature tends toward the good" is a self-evident principle only if one defines "the good" as "that toward which nature tends." Because in fact, nature tends just as readily—indeed, more readily—in the direction of dissolution, destruction, randomness, pain, and decay, as it does in the direction of building up, creativity, system, euphoria, and growth. Witness the second law of thermodynamics.

The point is that there is nothing in natural objects and their tendencies that would allow us to pick out some direction things "ought" to be taking; things just have tendencies. Even the law that all changes move from instability to equilibrium is just a statement of what always happens, because of the way scientists have defined terms (the "unstable" is what is moved away from). And this is why the "groaning of nature" is imposing a finality on nature as if it were God's, when in fact the Creator has no preference. If the Creator had a preference, the only way we could know is if he told us (which he did not, at least not unambiguously) or if he showed us by some inherent "natural" tendencies in things (which

2. For a defense of this interpretation, see my "The Meaning of 'Energia' and 'Entelechia' in Aristotle," 101–117.

just are not there in any preferential way). Is polluted air "groaning" to be clean? It has a tendency in that direction, under certain conditions. But it does not under other conditions, and in fact it can be in equilibrium as quite polluted. We do not like polluted air, but what evidence do we have to say that God does not, or that the air would rather be unpolluted?

Do not misunderstand me; I am not saying that it is bad to clean up the air. What I am saying is that we cannot say that the air is crying out to be cleaned. And if we clean it up, we are engaged in technological activity. But if we clean it up under the illusion that we are "helping it to be itself," we are the victims of the technical mentality-in the form of not recognizing the multiple finalities in things. Attributing some univocal finality to the world is no more to recognize it for what it really is than to deny it any finality at all. Put this another way: A Christian who longs to right the wrongs in the world is a Christian who has succumbed to the technical mentality. He places all the stress on efficient causality, ignores the finalities in the world, and ultimately succumbs to belief in his own omniscience. The Christian will do things that right the wrongs of the world; but this is an overflow of the Christian attitude he has, not the point of it, and ultimately the result of factors other than himself. The distinction is subtle, but crucial. Just as the Christian fulfills the whole law without being subject to it, so he does what is good, and in so doing corrects evil while he is at it, without necessarily trying to correct evil. To understand his action as carrying out some univocal tendency of the world would be to idolatrize the world.

But then what does one do to be Christian? One looks on the world in a new way. Christianity is *theoria par excellence.* The Christian has God's attitude toward things. And the reason I can say that the Christian is not essentially trying to correct the evils in the world is that from God's point of view, nothing is evil. God sees things as they are, not as they "ought" to be. If he saw them as they "ought" to be, this would mean that his view of their "true reality" would be what they "ought" to be, and he sees their actual reality as falling short of their "true" reality. But how can that "true reality" be true if it does not exist, did not exist, and never will exist? The true reality of anything is the way it is—and that is how God sees it. So God cannot see things as evil but only as being, and being capable of being other—as having potencies. But which potencies "ought" to be realized depends on what acts on them, or upon their free choices, not upon some preconceived scheme which can be thwarted.

God is perfectly happy with all the misery in this world—and even with the eternal misery of souls in hell.

Then what does the Christian do as Christian? Nothing specific, except be happy. Does he get involved in parish activities? Not necessarily. Does he give to the poor? Not necessarily. The Christian as Christian respects everything infinitely, and if he has this divine attitude, he is totally free from duties. He does not have to do anything; he does what he pleases. Life for him is not serious; it is a game—because the whole universe is not serious. In the eternal scheme of things, nothing is important because nothing "ought" to be a certain way. God is infinitely happy whatever the world chooses to make of itself, and so nothing can shake the happiness of the Christian. You say to him, "You can be happy having just lost your job and then broken your leg?" And he says, "What does it matter? God is happy."

But we so much want to turn Christianity into a plan for action, so that we can measure how Christian we are, and so we can find out whether our neighbor is living up to Christianity or not. And that, of course, is phariseeism, the very thing that Christ fulminated against. What importance does it have how far along in the spiritual life we are? And what possible significance for us can it have how far along some other person is?

2.

Many of us, I think, do not actually take our philosophy seriously enough in relation to our faith. If you take seriously the immutability and impassibility of God, both of which are established conclusions of philosophical theology, then God cannot be affected at all by anything that happens on earth. And God can have no other will for the earth than that which happens on it. He does not have a "permissive will" for the evil, as if he would rather that it did not happen. He might be said to have a hypothetical will for the evil in that he realizes that it did not have to happen, and the world would have been (in the abstract) better off if it had not; and if the world had chosen to go the better way, then that would have been his will for it. But by the same token, if the world had chosen something worse, that would have been his will also. There is a profoundly true sense in which it can and should be said that God does not care what happens in the world.

But does this not contradict the very essence of Christianity? If God does not care what we do, why did he die for us? Why did he redeem us? To ask "why" of a being who is absolutely complete is to ask a question that is fundamentally meaningless. He did it, certainly not because he was bothered by our sins, certainly not for some greater happiness he might have but—if you take the philosophy of God seriously—because he could. And it gives people a chance to escape the consequences of their sins, if they choose to take advantage of it. But if they do not, God is perfectly happy. It simply does not bother God if people go to hell.

Christianity shows how God loves us. He loves us enough so that he considers it of no importance to be God, but becomes a slave, and is obedient to death, even death on a cross (Philippians 2:5-8). His own reality does not matter to him. And this is the attitude that we are supposed to imitate. We are to consider our own reality of no importance whatsoever. The death of Jesus does not show us how important we are in God's eyes, just the opposite. It is supposed to show us—according not just to philosophy but to the Bible—how unimportant we ought to consider ourselves.

I find it fascinating that the philosophy of God as an all-perfect, completely self-sufficient being would lead logically to the conclusion that no creature has any importance for him and then be able to read in the Bible how we are to cultivate an attitude that we are not to consider ourselves important. We are to deny ourselves. Poverty is a blessing; those who do not stand up for their rights are admirable; we should enjoy being oppressed.[3] These enigmatic statements make sense if Christianity involves seeing the world as God sees it, and God sees it as philosophy says he has to.

That is, God created the world that it be what it is, not necessarily that it be headed somewhere. And since it remakes itself from within, you can say that he created it to make itself from within, and so his "plan" for the world, or his "purpose" for it, is for it to become whatever it makes itself to be. For it to do as it pleases to itself. It makes no difference to God if it turns out as what human beings call "bad" or "good."

But then if nothing matters, why bother acting at all? And the answer is the divine answer as to why God creates. Why not? An act does not have to have a purpose beyond itself to be meaningful; existence is intelligibility. And interestingly enough, to perform an act for no other

3. Matthew 5:3, 10–11, and 39–40; 1 Corinthians 6:7; and many other passages.

purpose than the act itself is the definition of having fun. So if we take the divine attitude toward our actions, realizing that nothing matters, then our whole life is meaningful, not for the sake of anything beyond it, but in itself—or our whole life is fun.

Seeing the world as groaning in labor is, as I see it, the very antithesis of the Christian attitude, and inevitably turns Christianity into a technique, where you are using God's greatest gift to the world for the sake of our petty purposes, like social justice, clean air, women's liberation, or whatever fad happens to be current. Instead of being free, we become—in the name of Christianity—slaves to a thousand duties and guilts. Instead of being happy and enjoying life, we become the grim custodians of hopeless causes, who can be thrown into despair by a synod of bishops, the election of Ronald Reagan, or the defeat of Ronald Reagan.

It is Christianity as technique where things matter so desperately that we will fight the Church when it says that contraception is wrong, where we will organize disobedience so that we can (we hope) force it to change its position, where we will adduce statistics to prove that we are right, and sneer when we are told that statistics do not make morality. It is Christianity as technique which keeps the schools open at the expense of decent salaries to the teachers, which engages in fraud to safeguard its doctrine, which fights opposition even to bloodshed. Christianity as technique has been with us a long time. Christianity as technique is a Christianity where things matter, where the good has to get done.

But things do not in fact matter, nor does any one of us matter, and since this is a fact, eventually we will have to face it. We will have to face the fact that the causes we fight for and we who fight for them are simply not of any importance whatever in the eternal scheme of things. And for those to whom it matters that they and their concerns do not objectively matter, this is hell. For those for whom such things do not matter, this is heaven.

Bibliography

Blair, George A. "The Meaning of 'Energia' and 'Entelechia' in Aristotle." *International Philosophical Quarterly* 7, no. 1 (March 1967) 101–117.

Essay 3

Through Christian Technology to Technological Christianity

Wilhelm E. Fudpucker, SJ

Modern man not only corresponds to Christianity's fundamental understanding of man but also . . . the historical breakthrough from theory to practice, from self-awareness to self-actualization was essentially a product of Christianity, however much many Christians opposed this emancipating movement of history.

—KARL RAHNER[1]

The idea that there is any inherent opposition between religion and technology founders on two brute facts: the historical reality that one particular religion, namely Christianity, has been the sponsor of modern technology, and the sociological truth that technology is creating a world which is manifestly more and more Christian. For Christianity, at least, there is no opposition to modern technology. Far from being opposed, the two are intimately, even mystically, intertwined. Christianity is both the Alpha and Omega of this-worldly practical action, the creative interface of orthodoxy and orthopraxis.

In support of this thesis I will argue, first, by a review of historical research and reflection, that Christian doctrine contains inherently technological predispositions; and second, by means of sociological analysis and projection, that technology is structuring a world which is

1. Rahner, *Theological Investigations* IX, 214.

objectively Christian and requires the exercise of Christian virtues. To anyone who complains that neither of these methods of argument is properly theological, I would quickly reply that Christianity (in contrast with all other religions) is both backward-looking (that is historical) and forward-looking (that is eschatological). History and futurology, as I shall use them, are distinctive products of a culture closely allied with the Christian world view.

1.

From the beginnings of conscious inquiry into the origins of modern technology the issue of Christian influence has been in the foreground. Max Weber's great work on *The Protestant Ethic and the Spirit of Capitalism* (1904–1905) established the terms for this debate regarding the relative importance of material and spiritual factors in the rise of modern economic and technological formations. But in maintaining the decisive influence of certain aspects of Christian spirituality, Weber reaffirms a viewpoint to be found at least as early as Francis Bacon (1561–1626) and in no less expansive a thinker than Georg Wilhelm Friedrich Hegel (1770–1831).

Bacon criticizes the barrenness of Aristotelian scholasticism precisely on the basis of an appeal to a compassionate pragmatism grounded in Christian moral principles. "By their fruits you shall know them." The pity with which the scientists of Bensalem (cf. Jerusalem) in the *New Atlantis* view the multitude is specifically modelled on Christ's compassion for the sick and hungry (*vide* Matthew 9:36, 14:14, and 15:32)—an emotion conspicuous by its absence among the philosophers of Athens. "Aristotle has not defined pity," proclaims Stephen Dedalus, "I have . . . . Pity is the feeling which arrests the mind in the presence of . . . human suffering and unites it with the human sufferer." It is no accident that James Joyce places such words in the mouth of a rebellious but well indoctrinated Catholic.[2]

Pity and the flight from suffering leads to the idea of freedom. Hegel, who regards Bacon and the Protestant mystic Jakob Böhme (1575–1624) as the twin founders of modernity, likewise clearly sees Christianity as playing a crucial role in the unfolding of freedom, which is the essence of world history. According to Hegel's philosophy of history: In the oriental

2. Joyce, *A Portrait of the Artist as a Young Man*, 204.

state only one man, the despot, is free. In Greek and Roman aristocracies, only a few men are free. But under the influence of Christianity men for the first time realize that man qua man is free. "This consciousness arose first in religion, the inmost realm of Spirit, but to introduce the principle into the various relations of the actual world, involves a . . . severe and lengthened process of culture."[3]

This dialectical process, by which the Christian ideal of freedom achieves worldly incarnation in the culture of the modern industrial state, itself divides into the three main periods of Christian history—according to the principle that later stages are always more differentiated than earlier ones. These three periods are the primitive, Catholic, and Protestant—which may, according to Hegel, also be likened to the Kingdoms of the Father, Son, and Holy Spirit. In the first, universal freedom is simply the other-worldly ideal of an undifferentiated ecclesiastical and secular realm; in the second or medieval period, religious is opposed to secular freedom; in the third, since the Reformation, the secular has been re-united to the ecclesiastical by being itself transformed with the principle of freedom. Although Hegel does not explicitly deal with technology as a key element in this transformation, a moment's reflection on the necessity of applied science to the realization of universal this-worldly freedom is enough to make the connection with Hegel's vision.

However, the most detail empirical evidence for the historical influence of Christianity on the development of modern technology is to be found in the work of Lynn White, Jr.—the single greatest historian of medieval technology. The over-riding focus of White's research—from *Medieval Technology and Social Change* (1962) to *Medieval Religion and Technology* (1978)—has been to document and explore the interrelationship between Christian culture and technology. The result has been that, against three quarters of a century of criticism of the Weber thesis, White has extended and vindicated it. For White the technological influence of Christianity does not begin with the Reformation, or even with monastic elements of the Middle Ages, but with the whole Christian worldview as it initiates a transformation of culture about the time of the Carolingian era.

In his first book White finds Christian attitudes toward the world manifested in the innovative adaptation of such devices as the stirrup, heavy plough, horseshoe and horse collar. The genius of Charles Martel

3. Hegel, *The Philosophy of History*, 18.

("Martel" means "hammer") in adapting an age-old device for steadying the leisure-rider or itinerate trader on his horse, to make possible mounted shock combat, was the basis of his decisive rout of the Muslims at Poitiers in 732 and subsequent Carolingian military power in eighth-century Europe. Together with the transformations in agriculture brought about by the heavy plough, horseshoe and collar, it made possible the feudal social system.

That such technological innovation was not simply accidental, White makes plain in "The Iconography of Temperantia and the Virtuousness of Technology" (1969). This classic of historical exegesis relies on manuscript illuminations and devotional traditions to argue that between the ninth and fifteenth centuries the invention and employment of technological instruments became recognized as a major element of the Christian spirituality. (Yankee ingenuity and the American love of gadgets is not just American, but Christian.) Temperance or discipline, which in more benighted times had been construed as one of the less exciting cardinal virtues was elevated to a dominant position and symbolized by technology. In White's words, "the idea of the rationally regulated life, which Weber rightly stressed as basic" to modern praxis became symbolized by the clock. "Then, toward the middle of the fifteenth century, Northern Europe clothed this supreme Virtue not simply with the clock but with the new technology of the later Middle Ages: on her head she wore the most complex mechanism of the era; her feet now rested on the most spectacular power engine of that generation; in her hands she held eyeglasses, the greatest recent boon to the mature literate man. The new icon of Temperance tells us that in Europe, below the level of verbal expression, machinery, mechanical power, and salutary devices were taking on an aura of "virtuousness" such as they have never enjoyed in any culture save the Western."[4]

Having documented this momentous shift in moral sensibility, White proceeds in "Cultural Climates and Technological Advance in the Middle Ages" (1971), to explore its causes. With the Marburg theologian, Ernst Benz, White identifies three major ones: From Genesis comes the idea of the world as a created artifact, revealing intelligent craftsmanship and design, and of man, created in the image of God, as called upon to participate with God in exercising dominion over creation. From Exodus

4. L. White, *Medieval Religion and Technology*, 201–202. The preceding quotation in the text is from p. 203. "Cultural Climates and Technological Advance in the Middle Ages" is also included in this collection.

comes the realization that history is not cyclical but linear, leading to a definite end, toward which man must contribute by means of his worldly activities. From the Gospels, and the dual doctrines of the Incarnation and Resurrection, comes the idea that matter is not evil but created for a spiritual purpose and destined for regeneration. Supplementing these, White mentions the Judeo-Christian de-animization of nature, and Christian moral concern for the material well-being of others—the latter being attested (although White does not catch this) by the rage for social justice among Old Testament prophets, as well as the healing and feeding miracles of Jesus.

White's theological speculations can easily be deepened. According to Herodotus, the Greeks are to be distinguished from the Egyptians by their ithyphallic—and therefore more human—art (*Histories* II, 60–61). According to Moses, the Jews are to be distinguished from the Egyptians by circumcision (Exodus 12:48). It is no doubt remarkable (if not symbolic) that each minority group chose the penis to point up its difference from the dominant people of the eastern Mediterranean area. But what is even more significant are the technological implications of circumcision over ithyphallic art. The latter leaves the penis exposed and in its natural state; the former surgically transforms it. Thus the idea that Jews or Christians should in any way be opposed to the further technological transformation of sex is as absurd as saying that they should be opposed to dams or insecticides.

Nowadays theological apologists often fall all over themselves trying to weasel out of the divine command to Adam (= "man") to "Be fruitful and multiply, and fill the earth and subdue it: and have dominion over the fish of the sea and over the birds of the air and over every living thing that moves upon the earth" (Genesis 1:28). But the Hebrew word translated here as "subdue" (*kabas*) is, if anything, even stronger than its standard English rendering; its basic meaning is "tread down" or "conquer," a meaning reinforced by the earlier use (Genesis 1:26) of radah, "trample," to express man's domination of the animals. Both terms clearly allude to man's primarily active and dominating role in creation—even foreshadowing the divine order to conquer Canaan and destroy all its inhabitants.

Remember, too, that when the Israelites flake out on the task of seizing this gift, they are severely punished. Yahweh is no candy-baby, and he does not expect anyone created in his image to be either—as is clear from the repetition of the divine command in Psalm 8 (to "fallen man," if you will) to take dominion over land, sea, and air. That modern technology should be absolutely necessary to the exercise of such power is obvious. The fact that many so-called religious leaders did not always see it this way (and often opposed technological progress) just exposes their own class bias and the dangers of a privileged elite. Remember that Jesus was not only the son of a *tekton* (Matthew 13:55), he was himself a *tekton* (Mark 6:3). St. Paul likewise practices a *techné* (Acts 18:3) and compares his work as an apostle to that of an *architekton* (1 Colossians 3:10; cf. Hebrews 11:10). Clearly, *techné* is not foreign to the Kingdom of God. When James Watt, President Reagan's Secretary of the Interior, says "My responsibility is to follow the Scriptures which call upon us to occupy the land until Jesus returns," he is expressing an eminently orthodox attitude denigrated by the ecological fear trips of faithless intellectuals.[5]

On the basis of some of his more popular presentations, White has sometimes been misread as rejecting Christianity. Certainly he has argued that Christianity is at the "historical roots of the ecologic crisis." In fact, however, although White admits that technological Christianity has engendered problems with which we must all now deal—problems which may indeed require us to re-evaluate elements of our Christian heritage—he does not in any way suggest that this should undermine the Christian tradition as a whole. Indeed, as is indicated in both his "historical roots" paper and elsewhere,[6] White seems to place hope in the inherent inventiveness of Christianity more than anything else. As Ortega y Gasset first pointed out in his marvelous *Meditación de la Técnica* (1939), what we need is not less but more invention, at the spiritual as well as the material level.

2.

The historical argument that Christianity has been inherently technological in its inner thrust and social influence is complemented by studies showing that the kind of social change which technology brings about—independent of any specific moral determination—is of such a character as to conform objectively to the most general and profound of Christian ideals. Indeed, as Walter Ong first observed a quarter century ago, on top

5. James Watt is quoted in Ajemian, "Zealous Lord of a Vast Domain," 27.

6. L. White, *Machina ex Deo,* "The Historical Roots of Our Ecologic Crisis." See also 55–64.

of the ever greater exercise of general Christian charity, belief is unmistakably more Catholic than it ever was in the so-called "age of faith."

> Today there are Catholics in every country of the globe . . . their lines of communication . . . are far more active and . . . their cohesion is more real than that of earlier Catholics . . . . The unique position of the Holy Father as head of the Church is much more obvious . . . . The faith has become more explicit on innumerable important points—many medieval Catholics, for example, felt quite convinced that Our Lady was conceived in original sin—and the faith has been disengaged from entanglements with errors of early physical science . . . . This kind of progress . . . going on within the interior of the Church herself suggests the impoverishment of the view which would interpret postmedieval history chiefly in terms of progressive "secularization" of everything and would see the development of modern science [and technology] which began in the sixteenth and seventeenth centuries . . . as . . . deplorable . . . . Seen in larger historical . . . perspectives, the age of technology is part of the great mysterious evolution of the universe devised by God.[7]

Needless to say there are always going to be specific aberrations or cases to the contrary. Nazi death camps and environmental pollution are no part of God's saving plan. But neither are they part of the essence of modern technology. They are aberrations that result when technology is deformed by pernicious political or economic interests. Freed from political constraints, engineers would never build instruments of destruction; liberated from economic demands, the technological eros for efficiency would reduce pollution to the point of insignificance. The technocracy movement espoused by Thorstein Veblen (1857–1929) was not far wrong; its dismissal by a profit-hungry right and rejection by left-wing "humanists" are equal tragedies of misconstrued self interest.

The radical leftist error of misplaced personalism is, however, the more grievous, because it aborted new historical conceptions. As Emmanuel Mounier (1906–1960), the original Christian personalist, argued with limpid resolve in *Be Not Afraid*, the disciple of Christ must not shirk his "demiurgic function" to recreate nature. Instead of indulging in facile romantic anathemas against the machine, he must recognize that "technical progress [is] an essential aspect of the Incarnation, and complete[s], on a certain level, the very Body of Christ." He quotes with

7. Ong, *Frontiers in American Catholicism*, 87–88.

approval Bergson's dicturn that "active mysticism [i.e., charity] . . . summons up the mechanical" as well as the more inconspicuous L. Malevez' s assertion that social progress "is an intrinsic aspect of the whole Christ, and a slow, mysterious elaboration of a new heaven and a new earth."[8] But for conspicuous and positive elucidation of the inner Christian essence of modern technology one must delve more deeply into the thought of two Jesuit theologians: Pierre Teilhard de Chardin and Walter Ong.

Teilhard is a man strongly influenced by Bergson, especially his *Creative Evolution* (1907). For Teilhard (1881–1955), science-technology and religion are but complementary approaches to one reality. The scientific description of reality (together with that technological praxis based on this knowledge of the laws of nature) reveals (and contributes to) an ordered or evolutionary change—geological merging into biological merging into societal evolution. From their beginnings, which are coeval with man, science and technology have conspired to create a planetary system of artifacts, a communications network destined to bring into existence a new level of human consciousness (the noosphere), whose effect can only adequately be described as the "hominization" of the earth. Religion, through its plumbing of the inner psychic depths, postulates by means of its eschatological-apocatastic elements and in the person of Christ a universal and egalitarian state free from want and fear. It is Teilhard's contention that this Omega point of global prosperity and peace is the same whether revealed by a phenomenology of the human presence in history or by theological exegesis. It must be; in the final analysis, there can be but one reality.

Such a proposition is confirmed by its illuminating power, as it enables one to return to the evolutionary drama and describe it in religious terms. This is the heart of Teilhard's great anthropological synthesis, *The Phenomenon of Man* (1965). The natural world operating according to the law of increasing complexity (cosmogenesis) engenders man; human action, especially of a scientific-technological character (anthropogenesis), creates the noosphere; within this spiritual realm a dynamism of hyper-personalism (Christogenesis) presses toward the culmination of history when the noosphere will break free from the planet giving birth to "the ultimate phenomenon of man."[9] The natural catapults into the

8. Mounier, *Be Not Afraid*, 49, 99. The first part of this volume, from which these quotations come, is a translation of La Petite peur du XXe siècle (Neuchâtel: Baconnière, 1948), which even rejects a negative interpretation of the atomic bomb

9. Teilhard, *The Phenomenon of Man*, 273. As an aside, I cannot help but complain

supernatural. When the weak-hearted Dominican Raymond Nogar complains that evolutionary action (and by implication human history as well) is more absurd than well-ordered, he is allowing himself to be overwhelmed by particulars.[10] When Martin Heidegger tells us that the essence of technology has not yet been thought,[11] he is only admitting is failure to read Teilhard or to know his alternative phenomenology of *Dasein*—a phenomenology more likely to grasp the meaning of Being because it focuses on man truly in the world, not just man's consciousness of being-in-the-world.

There has been much discussion of the methodology by which Teilhard arrives at and supports his conclusions. Teilhard himself insists he is not doing metaphysics but phenomenology, i.e., a careful attending to the phenomenon of the human in its logical relationship to all other phenomena. The logos so apprehended is what he calls a "law of complexification" in which "cosmic matter coils more and more closely in on itself." On the basis of this "physics" he builds, first, an apologetics which "identifies the Omega of reason with the Universal Christ of revelation," and, second, a mystique of action which leads one into a loving commitment to worldly involvement.[12] The most systematic attempt to draw out the personal, spiritual implications of his cosmic vision is contained in *The Divine Milieu* (1957).

But despite Teilhard's claims, it is clear that he does not have a deep attraction to the many details of the world, even though he certainly loves the world *qua* world; and it would be better to admit that he is more a prophet exercising his intuitions in a scientific poetry than a scientist *per se*. Only this, for instance, can account for his response to the problem of evil. For Teilhard was not, as he has sometimes been portrayed, a naive optimist. His early reflections on World War I, where the hideous

about the absolutely incredible fact that C. Mitcham and R. Mackey in their Bibliography of the *Philosophy of Technology* have completely ignored Teilhard—unless, of course, they have slotted him under someone else in their inimitable haphazard fashion. That Teilhard should not have been given major attention in the "Comprehensive" section of such a work is nothing short of scandalous—and calls the bibliographers' whole judgment into serious question.

10. Nogar, *The Lord of the Absurd.*

11. See Heidegger, *The Question Concerning Technology*, 3–49. That Heidegger admits the failure of even his own attempt to think technology is apparent from his remark on the bottom of page 23 and elsewhere.

12. See "Teilhard de Chardin's Thought," 148–149. Cf. also Teilhard's preface to *The Phenomenon of Man*, 29–30.

splendors of the front are compared to other catastrophic spectacles of evolution, are similar to those of Ernst Jünger's war dairy, *Storm of Steel*.[13] But whereas Jünger's reaction is transmuted by nihilism, Teilhard's is subsumed in faith. "The immense hazard and the immense blindness of the world are only an illusion to him who believes."[14]

Teilhard's cosmic vision is ably complemented by Walter J. Ong (1912–2003) and his more detailed phenomenological studies of the influence of communications technology on the structure of a cultural consciousness. With his late friend and confrere, Ong believes that "If Christ, in his human nature, is part of this world, then what this world is becomes a matter of immediate and profound theological meaning."[15] In a classic trilogy of studies in literary history—*The Presence of the Word* (1967); *Rhetoric, Romance, and Technology* (1971); and *Interfaces of the Word* (1977)[16]—Ong has explored what can be described as the three stages of noogenesis. These are cultures coordinate with three different types of communication: oral speech, written (chirographic and typographic) texts, and electronic media. Ong analyzes the internal characteristics of each form of culture, its specific noetic frameworks, the kinds of alienation that result with the advance from one to the other, and the reappropriations of the past that become possible as a result.

> The technological world is part of the human world . . . . Technology enters into consciousness more intimately than has commonly been thought, for the technologies of writing and print and electronic devices radically transform the word and

13. Compare Teilhard, *The Making of a Mind* with Jünger, *Storm of Steel*.

14. Teilhard, *The Divine Milieu*, 137. Note that this work on orthopraxis was composed much earlier (in the late 1920s) than his major work on orthodoxy (*The Phenomenon of Man*, from the late 1940s).

15. Ong, "Christian Values at Mid-Twentieth Century," 157.

16. In approaching these three works it is helpful to keep in mind two other aspects of Ong's literary output. He has published a number of collections of popular intellectual essays on contemporary Catholic culture, beginning with *Frontiers in American Catholicism* (1957) and including *The Barbarian Within* (1962) and *In the Human Grain* (1967). Here and in other uncollected popular pieces—such as "The Challenge of Technology," 21–24—he is most open about the faith that lies behind all his scholarly work. Ong also knows more about the pivotal sixteenth century rhetorician, Peter Ramus, than any other scholar, and has edited two collections of Ramus' work, plus written a classic two-volume study of Ramus and Ramusism: *Ramus, Method, and the Decay of Dialogue* (1958) and *Ramus and Talon Inventory* (1958). (The second volume is an extensive annotated bibliography on the works of Ramus and his disciple Omar Talon.)

> the mental processes which are the coefficients of speech and of which speech is the coefficient . . . . Writing grows out of oral speech, which can never be quite the same after writing is interiorized in the psyche . . . . Print grows out of writing and transforms the modes and uses of writing and thus also of oral speech and of thought itself. Electronic devices grow out of writing and print, and also transform writing and print, so that books of an electronic age can be distinguished, by their very organization of thought, from those of earlier ages.[17]

To offer one example of how this interaction between language technologies and consciousness plays itself out in history: In an oral-aural culture thought is necessarily episodic, formulary, yet always slightly different whenever it is repeated. The advent of writing introduces a new level of control, transforms episode into narrative, and allows linguistic formulas to atrophy. The new level of control makes greater analysis possible, which is extended when a chirographic culture invents the letterpress. "Before the invention of printing, logic manuals copied out in longhand had generally to content themselves with relatively simple spatial displays of terms, such as . . . the Porphyrian Tree . . . .With the invention of printing, it became feasible to include in the new mass-produced logic manuals not only this simple diagram but . . . much more elaborate spatial displays."[18]

As Werner Kelber has pointed out in an appreciative review of Ong's work, for Ong media do not control cultures in deterministic fashion. Instead, "each medium mobilizes ways of framing, shaping, and editing our vision, and successive media release psychic energy formerly untapped or locked in older forms of knowledge management."[19] In the age of electronic media such as radio and television, a new, "secondary orality" develops which is energized by transfusions from past media history toward an as yet unrealized apocatastic synthesis. Ong does not, however, leave this at the level of neutral description, but presents it as an

17. Ong, *Interfaces of the Word*, 339. One question I've always had when reading Ong: Why does he keep insisting on a tripartite division of this noogenetic history in which he has to artificially lump together chirographic and typographic cultures? He admits major differences between handwriting and moveable alphabetical typesetting cultures. Is it perhaps possible that his devotion to a three-stage history is controlled by the doctrine of the Trinity?

18. Ong, *Ramus, Method, and the Decay of Dialogue*, xv–xvi. This quotation comes from the commentary on an illustration.

19. Kelber, "Walter Ong's Three Incarnations of the Word," 73.

achievement in harmony with the inherent universality of the Christian message, the Christian bipolar appreciation of a divinely created world and the temporality of man's earthly home, and its person-centered understanding of God and man.

Consider briefly some aspects of these interrelated points. Many religions claim to be universal, but one has developed the technical capacity for truly universalizing itself. This increase in communications, through laden with responsibilities, is a multifaceted good. Over and over again Ong stresses how the great advances of knowledge have been dependent on technological forms of communication. The exploration of macro-distances (via telescope and spaceship) has proceeded alongside the penetration of micro-distances (via optical and electron microscope). The tools and techniques of archeo- and paleontology have probed the temporal recesses of human history. All this is stored and re-presented to each generation by a spectrum of means ranging from books to TV and word processers. Among world religions, moreover, Christianity is the only one which has developed a close alliance with secular (and international) learning. (Aberrations, such as the persecution of Galileo, are only remarkable against this backdrop. In Islam, Galileos have been persecuted thousands of times, not just once.) The Christian God is not a "god of the gaps," some fill-in for ignorance, but a god who is known because of his love for and association with the world, as its creator and redeemer. Knowledge, both scientific and technological, is a religious good.[20] "I am thinking God's thoughts after him," remarked Copernicus. None but a Christian scientist could make such a statement.

Appreciation of the temporality of the human lifeworld is intimately tied up with this cognitional dispensation and opens the Christian to participation in history in a way blocked to all non-Christians. As Mircea Eliade has argued with erudite display in *Cosmos and History: The Myth of the Eternal Return* (1954), all pagan religions are shot through with a terror of history and are structured as an escape from the ravages of time. Not so with Christianity. Its sacred scripture, the Bible, is neither an atemporal treatise on some spiritual science or technique (like the Upanishads) nor a literary narrative with "deep posteriority" (like a novel). The Bible as a whole (cf. the end of the Book of Revelation), as well as many of the books within it (cf. the Gospel of John, many Pauline letters, and even Deuteronomy) end not with some "they lived happily ever after"

20. See Ong, *In the Human Grain*, xi. On the unique Christian alliance with secular learning, see also Ong, *American Catholic Crossroads*, 137–139.

type formula, but with an opening into the future.[21] The Bible is unique in its account of a progressively unfolding salvation history, so much so that the modern idea of progress is unknown outside the Christian ambience.[22] Technology builds on and intensifies such an appreciation of temporality. "As man moves through time and his growth in knowledge accelerates, his relationship to time itself undergoes a change. He notices time more and more. He studies it and himself in it, becoming more and more explicitly knowledgeable about his past . . . . As knowledge of the past grows, focus on the present becomes more intent, for the present acquires a face of its own insofar as it can be both connected with and differentiated from the past circumstantially known. The knowledge explosion thus breeds the existentialist sensitivity to the present moment, felt as the front of past time, which marks our age."[23]

Finally, such existentialist sensitivity cross-bred with advances in communications technologies sprouts into a renewed alliance with the primacy of the personal, the very core of the Christian moral point of view. In a culture based on print, the eye takes over the dominant role exercised by the ear in an oral-aural culture. But vision inevitably depersonalizes. "In staring, one treats another person as an object. In speaking, one treats another person as a person. Sound relates to the interior dimensions of man. Sight relates merely to man's exterior."[24]

The advent of the telephone, phonograph, radio, TV and other electronic media thus bears a spiritual meaning in reacquainting man with the dimension of lived sound and the personal interaction with the lifeworld. To a student who once accused Ong of being a "flatterer of the age," Ong in effect replied that his faith would permit no other stance, and besides, the age deserves a bit of flattery. Technology is an anonymous Christianity waiting to be named.

3.

In conclusion, let me add a few personal remarks about the spiritual life in the presence of technology. Too often this is a subject approached only

21. See Walter J. Ong's critique of the Bible-as-literature idea in "Maranatha: Death and Life in the Text of the Book," in *Interfaces of the Word*, 230–271.

22. See Nisbet, *History of the Idea of Progress*.

23. Ong, *In the Human Grain*, x.

24. Ong, "The Spiritual Meaning of Technology and Culture," 30.

in negative terms, with recriminations about the destruction of bygone spiritual experiences, and with wistful longing for mystical detachment and contemplation. In many such discussions there seems to be an almost perverse attempt to ignore the way of mysticism in action—a way pointed to by Old Testament metaphors of God as artisan (cf. Wisdom 2:23–3:9 and 13:1–9, remembering, too, how man is said to be created in God's image) and explicitly espoused by Christ himself in the Beatitudes. Moreover, this is a spiritual path which, for those who need it, has been given an oriental blessing by Krishna in the Bhagavad Gita, and a medieval one by Richard of St. Victor when he speaks of the "fourth degree of passionate charity" in which "the soul goes forth on God's behalf."[25]

Admittedly, there have been some isolated attempts to appreciate this spiritual discipline of active mysticism. Friedrich Dessauer's almost wholly ignored vision of technology as a participation in divine creation is one case in point.[26] One is at pains to explain the almost embarrassed reaction to Dessauer's ideas even by engineers who in private admit to feeling such things in their hearts. Another, more widely discussed, is Harvey Cox's encomium to the spiritual benefits of the secular city, although he has since backtracked somewhat on his position.[27] Yet surely the contemporary effulgence of interest in all things spiritual—even the use of drugs and biofeedback techniques to make more accessible certain religious experiences (although, of course, these may sometimes be rather ersatz)—points in exactly the opposite direction, and toward the creative reappropriation of the past.

Andrée Bindewald, in a summary of her thesis on "Spiritual Living in a Technological Environment" (done under the much respected and even conservative Adrian van Kaam of Duquesne University), argues that despite all its dangers, "technology helps me to care effectively." "The new technological man emerging from today's culture participates in the environment, suffers with it, stands in dread of it, marvels at it, listens to mystery through it, redeems it. He is actively caring toward his environment and also contemplative toward it . . . . He lives in his material world while maintaining a vision of the future. He lives out of the integration of the body—spirit he is."[28]

25. See Happold, *Mysticism*, 100–104 and 241–248.

26. See Dessauer, *Philosphie der Technick*. A partial English translation miraculously made its way into Mitcham and Mackey's *Philosophy and Technology*.

27. See Cox, *The Secular City*. Cox's big retreat is *Feast of Fools*.

28. Bindewald, "Technology and Man's Future," 45. The preceding quotation is

In laying out the themes for a spirituality appropriate to the present—a synthesis of action and contemplation in the world that integrates both body and spirit—such a passage points toward a stance represented most fully in the spirituality of St. Ignatius of Loyola (1491–1556), as it was first formulated by a wounded soldier at the beginning of the age of modern technology. For St. Ignatius, too, it was important not to flee from the world in monastic fashion, but to remain as a determined actor who uses his active imagination to energize spiritual faculties. "Act as if it all depends on you; pray as if it all depends on God." The most vigorous action is united with the most intense prayer. Surely it is no accident that the principles Ignatius developed to guide the Society of Jesus have made that community both the single largest order of the Catholic Church in the modern world and given it the reputation of being the home of the "shock troops of the Pope." In the words of a great contemporary son of Loyola, the Christian must "march on unarmed through the ineffable dangers of the future of the world."[29]

But in an even more telling argument, the theologian, Arthur Gibson, having criticized the attitudes toward the future of thinkers as diverse as Charles Reich (rebellion), Arthur Koestler (detached veto), and Alvin Toffler (creative collaboration), writes of a fourth possibility.

> Man can freely opt to submit himself to technological organisms as their junior partner in a symbiosis that will transform them and him. Before the Creator, say all religious traditions, we are all ultimately passive even in the full exercise of our legitimate and inescapable freedom. Once that Creator called by a burning bush, a pillar of cloud by day and fire by night, but always to a humble yet courageous following of the Other. Today he calls via the phenomenon of man's own creature, technology, which has surpassed man. A loving and creative abandon will not destroy man's dignity but ensure the continuation of man's transformation, for "it had not yet appeared what we shall be!"[30]

Personally, I know of no more moving intimation of the deepest meaning of the Jesuit vow of obedience—when considered in light of the present stage of world history. To become servants of technology

---

from page 44.

29. Rahner, *Zur Theologie der Zukunft*, 113. This selection from Rahner's on-going *Schriften zur Theologie* includes material especially from Part Three of *Theological Investigations* VIII.

30. Gibson, "Visions of the Future," 118–126.

and its promises we are called, as if by God himself. *Ad majorem Dei gloriam*. Technology not only comes forth from Christianity, it takes us into Christianity in a new and fuller sense. Our personal obligation is to affirm that promise—and not, like Caleb's companions, to fear Canaan as a land filled with giants we cannot master.

Bibliography

Ajemian, Robert. "Zealous Lord of a Vast Domain." *Time*, March 30, 1981.

Bindewald, Andrée "Technology and Man's Future: Integrating Body and Spirit." *Humanitas* 14, no. 1 (February 1978) 31–46.

Cox, Harvey G. *Feast of Fools*. Cambridge, MA: Harvard University Press, 1969.

Dessauer, Friederich. *Philosphie der Technick*. Bonn: Ernst Klett Verlag, 1927.

Gibson, Arthur. „Visions of the Future." In *Humanism and Christianity*, edited by Claude Geffre, 118–126. New York: Herder & Herder, 1973.

Happold, F. C. *Mysticism: A Study and an Anthology*. Baltimore: Penguin, 1970.

Hegel, Georg Wilhelm Friedrich. *The Philosophy of History*. Translated by J. Sibree. New York: Dover, 1956.

Heidegger, Martin. *The Question Concerning Technology and Other Essays*. Translated by William Lovitt. New York: Harper & Row, 1977.

Joyce, James. *A Portrait of the Artist as a Young Man*. New York: Viking, 1964.

Jünger, Ernst. *Storm of Steel*. Garden City, NY: Doubleday, 1929.

Kelber, Werner H. "Walter Ong's Three Incarnations of the Word: Orality, Literacy, Technology." *Philosophy Today* 23, no. 1 (Spring 1979) 70–74

Mounier, Emmanuel. *Be Not Afraid: A Denunciation of Despair*. London: Rockliff, 1951.

Nogar, Raymond J., OP. *The Lord of the Absurd*. New York: Herder & Herder, 1966.

Ong, Walter J. *American Catholic Crossroads: Religious-Secular Encounters in the Modern World*. New York: Macmillan, 1959.

———. *The Barbarian Within, and Other Fugitive Essays and Studies*. New York, Macmillan, 1962.

———. "The Challenge of Technology." *Sign*, February 1968. 21–24.

———. "Christian Values at Mid-Twentieth Century." *Theology Digest* 4, no. 3 (Autumn 1956) 155–157.

———. *Frontiers in American Catholicism*. New York: Macmillan, 1957.

———. *In the Human Grain*. New York: Macmillan, 1967.

———. *Interfaces of the Word: Studies in the Evolution of Consciousness and Culture*. Ithaca: Cornell University Press, 1977.

———. *Ramus, Method, and the Decay of Dialogue*. Cambridge, MA: Harvard University Press, 1958.

———. *Ramus and Talon Inventory*. Cambridge, MA: Harvard University Press, 1958.

———. "The Spiritual Meaning of Technology and Culture" In *Technology and Culture in Perspective*, edited by Myron B. Bloy, Jr. and Ilene Montana, 29-34. Cambridge, MA: Church Society for College Work, 1967.

Rahner, Karl. *Theological Investigations IX: Writings of 1965–67*. Translated by Graham Harrison. New York: Herder & Herder, 1972.

———. *Zur Theologie der Zukunft*. Munich: Deutscher Taschenbuch, 1971.

Teilhard de Chardin, Pierre. *The Divine Milieu*. New York: Harper & Row, 1960.

———. *The Making of a Mind: Letters from a Soldier-Priest 1914–1919*. New York: Harper & Row, 1965.

———. *The Phenomenon of Man*. Translated by Bernard Wall. New York: Harper & Row, 1959.

———. "Teilhard de Chardin's Thought as Written by Himself." In Abbé Paul Grenet, *Teilhard de Chardin: The Man and His Theories*, 148–149. New York: Paul S. Erikson, 1966.

White, Lynn, Jr. *Machina Ex Deo: Essays in the Dynamism of Western Culture*. Cambridge, MA: MIT Press, 1968.

———. *Medieval Religion and Technology: Collected Essays*. Berkeley: University of California Press, 1978.

———. *Medieval Technology of Social Change*. New York: Oxford University Press, 1962.

Essay 4

Bernard Lonergan: A Context for Technology

Terry J. Tekippe

Bernard Lonergan has no book or even article exclusively devoted to technology; while his perspective on it is interesting, it may be safely assumed that in his comments, always more or less in passing, he will not have much entirely new or original to offer. But what Lonergan generally excels in is plumbing the deeper epistemological, philosophical and theological dimensions of a topic; and in this particular case, he contributes a larger framework or context within which to view technology. What follows will therefore outline Lonergan's notion of technology and then show how its implications fit into his whole system. To many readers, however, Lonergan may require a prior introduction—which will be provided by an opening section.

Who is Bernard Lonergan?

Lonergan is a contemporary philosopher and theologian,[1] a Jesuit priest, who was born in Canada, taught theology there and at the Gregorian University in Rome for many years, and presently is teaching and writing in the United States. In 1979 he celebrated his seventy-fifth birthday.

A "theologian's theologian," Lonergan is not very well known outside a narrow circle; his work is anything but popular, concentrating rather on

1. Editor's Note: Bernard Lonergan died in 1984, not long after the original printing of this work.

the most abstruse questions of theological procedure. His lifelong interest has been theological method, and its fruits are evident in his *Method in Theology* (1972), but perhaps his most brilliant and lasting contribution is found in the philosophical background he worked out for his theological approach: *Insight: A Study of Human Understanding* (1957).

Lonergan takes his philosophical stand in the Aristotelian-Thomist tradition; yet his approach meshes congenially with modern philosophy, especially in its Kantian variations. A word must be said on these antecedents if Lonergan is to be helpfully situated in the philosophical tradition.

Plato and Aristotle are the two great authors who initiated the Western philosophical project. Especially as their schools and adherents developed in the later philosophical tradition, they have often been opposed as two separate and eternally distinct ways of doing philosophy, so that any later philosopher will inevitably be either a Platonist or an Aristotelian. That there is a great deal of truth in this typology cannot be denied, but that the two have much in common should also not be overlooked. Aristotle is, after all, Plato's star pupil, and he retains much of his master's doctrine, methodology, presuppositions and enthusiasms. Aristotle can often be read as merely taking to their logical conclusion trajectories initiated by Plato.

Nevertheless, characteristic differences remain, and the distinctive Aristotelian style is of interest here. Aristotle is determinedly and pervasively scientific, in the sense of heading toward a precise, systematic and overwhelmingly logical presentation of every area he investigates. He does not, in fact, produce a fully-rounded, internally coherent, systematic account of reality; but there is enough of the theory of it, and a sufficient number of the pieces gathered together, to offer a good approximation. Aristotle is largely responsible for firing the imagination of the West with the ideal and the vision of complete scientific explanation.

Plato evidences a quite ambivalent position on myth. On the one hand, he wants to exclude the poets from his ideal republic, but at the same time, he himself uses myth to vivid and telling effect in his dialogues. But Aristotle is truer to Plato's own theory and rigorously expels myth from his writings. Rhetoric, which persuades, is a mode of speech far inferior to science, which demonstrates. Aristotle's presentation, accordingly, is dry, abstract, logical, yet such speech has exerted its own compelling, if austere, fascination upon the Western philosophical tradition.

In spite of a highly abstract presentation, Aristotle remains very concrete, and even empirical, in his approach to reality. Against Plato, who located the really real beyond the shifting realm of sense knowledge, Aristotle firmly insists that all knowing begins in the senses. Plato concentrates on the supersensible Forms; Aristotle grounds the form within the individual, material existent. Aristotle displayed a permanent interest in collecting and cataloguing, whether it was marine biological specimens or the constitutions of various states. In short, Aristotle's logical, rigorous, down-to-earth and concrete temper would make him a comfortable companion to the contemporary scientist. One of the ironies of the history of Western philosophy is that modern science imaged itself as precisely a revolt against the Aristotelians.

Thomas Aquinas, it may be said, took up precisely where Aristotle left off—a statement that possesses some degree of historical accuracy, in that Plato and Aristotle found no worthy successors in the Greek tradition, and Plato was the reigning master in Christianity from the third to the twelfth century.[2] When Thomas was a young student, Aristotelianism was rolling into Europe like the wave of the future; Thomas mastered his patrimony early, grasped its potential contribution to a scientific statement of Christian reality, and spent his life recasting the theological tradition of the Church Fathers and the early Scholastics into an Aristotelian mold. In some seventeen years of furious writing, he commented perspicaciously on the most important Aristotelian works and brought the new literary form of the synthetic *summa* to a comprehensiveness and logical articulation as yet unknown.

As may be expected, the resultant theological statement is logical, precise, scientific. Shriven of any emotion, it subordinates conclusions to principles with the rigor of a computer program. The advantage of such an austere mode of thought is scope: the intellectual vision roams from man to nature to angels to God, finding analogies throughout, employing a small number of principles with suppleness and yet consistency to bind the whole into a unity. Few have attempted system-building on the scale that Thomas did. That is another of the ironies of Western philosophy: when reason was most subordinate as the handmaid of faith, it disported most freely through all the realities of earth and heaven; no sooner did it proclaim its independence in the Enlightenment than, especially in Kant, it straightway begins to set limits to itself.

2. A fuller account, however, would have to include the Arabic contribution, in its transmission of and commentary upon the Aristotelian corpus.

Medieval thought, especially in Thomas, was decidedly objective; emotion and desire were pushed aside to attain the high abstraction of complete scientific statement. Descartes begins modern thought with a turn to the subject: I think, therefore I am. Not that he desired to be any less scientific: his appeal to the *Cogito* had as motive precisely the discovery of an indubitable and immovable basis upon which to erect a rigorous logical expansion. Nevertheless, a die had been cast; the subject was imported into philosophy with consequences as yet unforeseen. Kant not only continues but expands this turn to the subject; he calls for a Copernican revolution, in which the object should revolve around the subject, rather than the subject around the object. Where Descartes turned to the self only long enough to set the foundation for his philosophical system, Kant proposed a new science of criteriology, the self-knowledge of knowledge, which would rigorously, and once for all, examine knowing to discover its structure, virtualities and limitations.

In light of this background, Lonergan may now be presented as a neo-Kantian neo-Thomist. He accepts with enthusiasm the Cartesian turn to the subject; more specifically, he embraces the Kantian program of a prior inquiry into knowing, so that his cognitional analysis issues into a critical epistemology, and the epistemology into a metaphysics. Lonergan envisions this prior inquiry as an empirical one; it is based, not on what knowing should or must be, but on what it is in fact found to be. Only, where physical science turns outward to the world to discover its givens, cognitional analysis turns inward, to focus on the data of consciousness. Lonergan's only disagreement with Kant is over the precise structure, virtualities and limitations of human knowing.

When Lonergan in fact catalogues the operations and activities of knowing, from them develops a normative epistemology, and then extends this into a metaphysics, he finds that his conclusions coincide very closely to the metaphysical vision of Aristotle and Thomas. Yet Lonergan sees this advantage to his approach to philosophy through the prior, Kantian-style examination of knowing: he is able to point to an empirical basis for his position. Ultimately, every metaphysical assertion can be traced back to its ground in the cognitional analysis; and since that analysis is an empirical one, founded on the facts of knowing as they are concretely discovered to be, then metaphysics is afforded an empirical and scientific basis. Thus Lonergan understands his achievement to be the grounding of the Aristotelian-Thomist metaphysics on a new and empirically verifiable basis.

Lonergan's View of Technology

Thomas Aquinas' view of reality is a thoroughgoing intellectualist one; hence it is not surprising that Lonergan's understanding of technology focuses on its intellectual aspects. Technology begins with the idea of an inventor. What the inventor knows is not some already existing reality; it is an idea of what may become a reality if certain conditions are met: if financial support is found, if a working model proves out, if market conditions are favorable.[3] Even when the product is realized, it remains precisely the realization of an idea, and so technology may be viewed as a kind of meaning. Lonergan envisions the American plain as Columbus discovered it, and then compares it with intervening achievement: it has been divided into plots, crisscrossed with roads, populated with cities, dotted with factories. All of this may be seen as the imposition of a meaning upon a previous potentiality.[4] Put negatively, without meaning there would be no technology; all human institutions, in fact, would disappear.[5] Technology even creates a new language in which to express itself. "The long transition from primitive fruit-gatherers, hunters, and fishers to the large-scale agriculture of the temple states and later the high civilizations brought with it a vast enrichment of language. For men do not do things without first talking about them and planning them, and so there had to be a linguistic development equal to the great works of irrigation, the vast structures of stone or brick, the armies and navies, the complicated processes of bookkeeping, and the beginnings of arithmetic, geometry and astronomy."[6]

Technology, of course, is a knowing concerned with doing and making; inevitably, it changes the world in which man lives. Technology creates a product that intervenes between man and nature; through it, man creates for himself an artificial environment. This creation of a technological product and the distancing of man from nature is in turn, however, the making of man, who comes to self-realization, at least partially, by contemplating the tools of his making.[7] But what Lonergan is above all concerned to underline is that, even as product, technology continues to reside, more than all else, in the minds and wills of people. Technology

3. Lonergan, *Verbum*, 5.

4. Lonergan, *Method in Theology*, 78.

5. Lonergan, *Bernard Lonergan: 3 Lectures*, 38.

6. Lonergan, *Philosophy of God*, 2–3.

7. Lonergan, *Insight*, 536.

has a home not only in the mind of the inventor, but also in the skill of the worker who utilizes the machine, the manager who sets him to his work, the entrepreneur who raises the capital to employ both worker and manager. As Lonergan points out, "A vast technological expansion, robbed of its technicians, would become a monument more intricate but no more useful than the pyramids."[8]

Lonergan distinguishes various areas or kinds of knowing: aesthetic knowing, theoretical knowing, religious knowing, and practical or common sense knowing. It is usually in the last category that Lonergan classifies technology.[9] Common sense knowing is the pattern of experience familiar to everyone, the one in which a child grows up. It concerns itself with the practical world of doing and making, of eating, sleeping and mating, of food, shelter and clothing. It is the pragmatic world of the businessman, the worker; it never strays far from concrete goods and services into the abstract world of theory. Men of common sense are busy about work of the world; they have little time to spend on high-flown speculations.[10] As society becomes more complex, it tends to differentiate into several specialties; then the farmer had better mind his cows, and the shoemaker stick to his last if either is to know what he is doing. Technological knowledge is a further specialization of common sense, arising in more complex societies; but with all common sense, it is concerned with proximate goals of doing and making.

Nevertheless technology has as well its theoretical component, and in other statements Lonergan presents it, more completely, as the child of both common sense and theoretical-scientific knowing.

> If the domains of science and common sense are distinct, so also they are complementary. If one must recognize the differences in their objects, their criteria, their universes of discourse, their methodological precepts, one must also insist that they are the functionally related parts within a single knowledge of a single world. The intelligibility that science grasps comprehensively is the intelligibility of the concrete with which common sense deals effectively. To regard them as rivals or competitors is a

8. Lonergan, *Insight*, 210.

9. Lonergan's technical use of term "common sense" and his discussion of how it merges with science to produce technology apparently develops an argument made by Alexandre Koyré in "Dur Monde de l'à peu près a l'Univers de la Precision," 806–823—a review article dealing with Lewis Mumford's *Technics and Civilization*.

10. Lonergan, *Insight*, 173–181.

> mistake, for essentially they are partners and it is their successful cooperation that constitutes applied science and technology, that adds inventions to scientific discoveries, that supplements inventions with organizations, know-how, and specialized skills.[11]

Aristotle distinguished sharply between science, which contemplates the universal and the necessary, and prudence and art, which deal with the changeable and accidental worlds in which human doing and making take place. This dichotomy, in the contrast of the lonely researcher, who cares but to know, and the applied scientist, who adapts the abstract theories, still retains a contemporary resonance. But in fact, the whole notion of science has changed since Aristotle's time: it is hypothetical, not necessary, and provisional, not eternally valid, and consequently the gap between theory and practice is no longer so wide. "Aristotle, then, was quite right in holding that a science that consisted in the grasp of necessary truth had to be purely theoretical and could not be practical. But from the start modern science intended to be practical. Today there are many steps along the way from basic research to pure science, from pure science to applied, from applied to technology, from technology to engineering. But the multiplicity does not obscure the underlying unity. For us good theory is practical, and good practice is grounded in sound theory."[12]

Technology, then, arises from the mating of theoretical science and common-sense concerns. Like technology, science exists above all in the minds of scientists. Further, no science can exist in its completeness in any one mind; science is a social possession. "No individual knows the whole of modern mathematics, or the whole of physics, or the whole of chemistry, or the whole of biology. Such knowledge is possessed not by an individual but by members of a group."[13]

To this point, the analysis of technology has been rather static, but one of the most egregious aspects of technology, of course, is its dynamism. Each generation takes the achievement of the previous one to build on; the expansion is unending, and, in fact, increases at an exponential rate. Lonergan recognizes such development, but in keeping with his distinctive viewpoint, he envisions it as precisely a growth of intelligence.

11. Lonergan, *Insight*, 297–298.

12. Lonergan, "The Ongoing Genesis of Methods," 343.

13. Lonergan, "The Ongoing Genesis of Methods," 342–343.

> Moreover, such an intervention of intelligence is itself recurrent. As products of human ingenuity, spears and nets illustrate not only the idea of the old mechanical arts but also the more recondite idea of modern technology. As pieces of material equipment, the same objects are initial instances of the idea of capital formation. Now the history of man's material progress lies essentially in the expansion of these ideas. As inventions accumulate, they set problems calling for more inventions. The new inventions complement the old to suggest further improvements, to reveal fresh possibilities and, eventually, to call forth in turn the succession of mechanical and technological higher viewpoints that mark epochs in man's material progress.[14]

As a result, intelligence plays a more and more preponderant role in technology. In its early stages, technology depends heavily on external conditions, the availability of materials, and so on. But as it advances, it becomes more and more a function of the occurrence or nonoccurrence of the appropriate insights. Whitehead liked to reflect that the Romans had all the technical abilities and the materials to build a steam engine. Why did they not do so? Because no one had the leisure to contemplate a tea pot and dream of the possibilities of steam power.

If technology grows with time, it also spreads out in space, or geographically. Good ideas cannot be tied down. Trade and the profit motive have little respect for artificial boundaries. Consequently, technical inventions spread, often rather rapidly, over great distances. "Material and social progress refuses to be confined to a single country; like an incoming tide, first it reaches the promontories, then it penetrates the bays, and finally it pours up the estuaries. In an intricate pattern of lags and variations, new ideas spread over most of the earth to bind together in an astounding interdependence the fortunes of individuals living disparate lives in widely separated lands."[15]

With the foregoing ideas, Lonergan's notion of progress may now be presented. Progress is the beneficent effect of creative intelligence. At each stage of humankind's progress, creative intelligence grasps the needs of human living, the resources available, the technical possibilities of utilizing them, the practical steps necessary to realize the inventions, the policies and social structures requisite for such realization. The new products and organizations largely improve the situation: what

14. Lonergan, *Insight*, 208.

15. Lonergan, *Insight*, 214.

oversights and failures occur are rapidly corrected by a further exercise of creative intelligence, and the better human situation in turn suggests still better products and policies. "Thus, insight into insight brings to light the cumulative process of progress. For concrete situations give rise to insights which issue into policies and courses of action. Action transforms the existing situation to give rise to further insights, better policies, more effective courses of action. It follows that if insight occurs, it keeps recurring; and at each recurrence knowledge develops, action increases its scope, and situations improve."[16]

The Worm in the Apple

If nothing more were said, Lonergan's notion of progress would seem dangerously naive. What beneficent recurrence of insight is it, for example, which gives birth to the hydrogen bomb? Is not the advance of knowledge a two-edged sword? Lonergan responds also to these questions, and the answer continues to be in terms of intelligence.

Besides insight, besides the drive to know which brings about insight, a flight from understanding is also evident in human affairs. At first blush, this may seem a strange notion-who would deliberately want not to understand? Yet on second thought, it proves not so farfetched. Many persons will go to strenuous lengths to avoid knowing themselves as they really are, and they may be quite angry with anyone who decides to favor them with a look at their real selves. Again, everyone is familiar with work or social situations where obvious improvements almost cry out for implementation. Why are they not effected? The reason may range from laziness to obtuseness to incompetence to greed to petty privilege to hidebound traditionalism to resentment to cynicism. The result is the same: a refusal of insight, the consequent neglect of fruitful and timely ideas, and the transmission to the next generation of mutilated and incoherent ideas.[17]

The motivations for the flight from understanding Lonergan analyzes more technically under the notion of biases. First is individual bias, the distortion introduced into knowing by an unfortunately all-too-familiar egoism. The egoist exploits intelligence to descry his utmost personal advantage, but then he refuses to face the further question of what his

16. Lonergan, *Insight*, xiv.

17. Lonergan, *Insight*, 229, 233.

advantage will mean for the common good. Thus, individual bias leads to a flight from understanding on the group or social level. But a group bias also exists. Then a group similarly exploits intelligence to maximize its own fortunes and position. Once again, however, the further questions are balked because insights into the good of a larger group might prove uncomfortable or costly. So pressure groups are concerned about their own pet interests, to the detriment of the national interest; and nations seize their own opportunities, oblivious to the repercussions on the human family as a whole.

But these are not the most virulent biases; individual bias tends to cancel out against the competing egoism of other individuals. Groups, too, meet the opposition of other groups; later, if not sooner, the oppressed group will rise up to take its vengeance on the dominant group. No, the worst bias is what Lonergan terms the bias of common sense itself: the tendency of common sense to seek its short-term, immediate, practical and palpable good, while failing to advert to the deeper question of real or long-term practicality. To face such larger and more intricate questions, unfortunately, common sense knowing has neither the patience nor the technical qualifications. Common sense

> is concerned with the concrete and the particular. It entertains no aspirations about reaching abstract and universal laws. It is easily led to rationalize its limitations by engendering a conviction that other forms of human knowledge are useless or doubtfully valid. Every specialist runs the risk of turning his specialty into a bias by failing to recognize and appreciate the significance of other fields. Common sense almost invariably makes that mistake; for it is incapable of analyzing itself, incapable of making the discovery that it too is a specialized development of human knowledge, incapable of coming to grasp that its peculiar danger is to extend its legitimate concern for the concrete and the immediately practical into disregard of larger issues and indifference to long-term results.[18]

Technology, as seen already, is basically a common sense kind of knowing. Hence it will share the characteristics of common sense knowing and be subject to its peculiar bias. But the result is that technology, and its impact on human history, will be involved in the long-term incoherencies to which common sense is prone.

18. Lonergan, *Insight*, 226.

> But the general bias of common sense prevents it from being effective in realizing ideas, however appropriate and reasonable, that suppose a long view or that set up higher integrations or that involve the solution of intricate and disputed issues. The challenge of history is for man progressively to enlarge the realm of conscious grasp and deliberate choice. Common sense accepts the challenge, but it does so only partially. It needs to be guided but it is incompetent to choose its guide. It becomes involved in incoherent enterprises. It is subjected to disasters that no one expects, that remain unexplained even after their occurrence, that can be explained only on the level of scientific or philosophic thought, that even when explained can be prevented from recurring only by subordinating common sense to a higher specialization of human intelligence.[19]

As insight tends to be recurrent and cumulative, giving rise to progress, so the flight from understanding is also a successive devolution. This is what Lonergan terms decline. "Similarly, insight into oversight reveals the cumulative process of decline. For the flight from understanding blocks the insights that concrete situations demand. There follow unintelligent policies and inept courses of action. The situation deteriorates to demand still further insights and, as they are blocked, policies become more unintelligent and action more inept. What is worse, the deteriorating situation seems to provide the uncritical, biased mind with factual evidence in which the bias is claimed to be verified. So in ever increasing measure intelligence comes to be regarded as irrelevant to practical living."[20]

These last observations deserve to be spelled out in more detail. Were world history simply a matter of creative intelligence and progress, then a smooth upward curve would result. But to the extent that the flight from understanding and the refusal of insight occur, human history is much more ambivalent. It is a pattern of light and darkness, a series of jerks and starts and stops, an incoherent mixture of creative understanding and of fearful flight from understanding.

If intelligence creates a meaning in technology, if technology intervenes between man and nature so as ultimately to affect man's understanding of himself, then the result of the injection of the refusal to understand is bound to be a marred meaning, an incoherent situation,

19. Lonergan, *Insight*, 228.

20. Lonergan, *Insight*, xiv.

and ultimately a faulty self-understanding. The human situation at any one time is a composite of the meaning and non-meaning previously introduced into it. Lonergan compares it to the complex variable of mathematics; the social situation possesses a real component (the fruit of insight) and a surd (the incoherencies of refusal to understand).

Once again, the implications are cumulative. For the human situation at any one time is not only the product of previous human creation or destruction, but also the occasion for any further human decision and action. To the extent a situation is incoherent, it is likely to suggest only incoherent remedies; when these are adopted, then the situation becomes still worse.

Eventually, insight and intelligence will seem to be more and more irrelevant to such a murky and incoherent situation. Consequently, they will be ridiculed as "hopelessly idealistic" or "utopian." What is likely to follow is that intelligence and reasonableness will themselves despair and come to an uneasy compromise by proposing to deal with just the "facts" of the concrete situation, never mind whether those facts are coherent or incoherent. At such a juncture, there is lacking the only agent—creative intelligence—which might have found an intelligent way out of the impasse; the social surd grows like a tumor, and the human situation sinks into a rather rapid decline.[21]

The use of force, it may be noted, offers no solution to this dilemma. Within limits, force can be used against more extreme cases of individual bias. But there is a limit to how many persons can be put in jail or coerced by the law. If egoism becomes too widespread, then force and law will themselves have to bend and compromise.[22] To use force against groups is even trickier, particularly when they are large and powerful. What usually happens, instead, is that the dominant group subtly or even boldly captures the forces of law and order to impose them on the oppressed minority. Finally, the use of force is least of all useful in countering the bias of common sense. First, because everyone is subject to the influence of this bias, and force cannot be used against all; second, because the bias is basically a flight from understanding, and force is a poor instrument to help people understand. What usually happens, rather, is that the use of blind force quickly allies itself with the worst forms of the flight from understanding. "Finally, if force can be used by the group against

21. Lonergan, *Insight*, 229–232.

22. Lonergan, *Second Collection*, 54.

the wayward individual and by the larger group against the smaller, it does not follow that it can be used to correct the general bias of common sense. For the general bias of common sense is the bias of all men and, to a notable extent, it consists in the notion that ideas are negligible unless they are reinforced by sensitive desires and fears. Is everyone to use force against everyone to convince everyone that force is beside the point?"[23]

Decline is cumulative, then, and the use of force is unavailing to counter it. The result is that the objective human situation progressively deteriorates.

> Increasingly the situation becomes, not the cumulative product of coherent and complementary insights, but the dump in which are heaped up the amorphous and incompatible products of all the biases of self-centered and shortsighted individuals and groups. Finally, the more the objective situation becomes a mere dump, the less is there any possibility of human intelligence gathering from the situation anything more than a lengthy catalogue of the aberrations and the follies of the past. As a diagnosis of terminal cancer denies any prospect of health restored, so a social dump is the end of fruitful insight and of the cumulative development it can generate.[24]

In keeping with Lonergan's distinctive viewpoint, however, it is important to emphasize once more that the social surd is found only secondarily in the objective human situation; in a primary sense, it exists in the minds and wills of men.

> If this succession of ever less comprehensive syntheses can be deduced from man's failure to understand himself and his situation dialectically, if historically evidence for the failure and its consequences is forthcoming both in the distant and in the recent past, still it is far too general a theorem to unravel at a stroke the tangled skein of intelligibility and absurdity in concrete situations. Its generality has to be mediated by a vast accumulation of direct and inverse insights and by a long series of judgments of truth and of value, before any concrete judgments can be made. And on what Galahad shall we call to do the understanding and to make the judgments? For the social surd resides least of all in outer things and most of all in the minds and wills of men. Without an unbiased judge, the truth would not be reached; and if an unbiased judge were found, would the

23. Lonergan, *Insight*, 632.

24. Lonergan, *Bernard Lonergan: 3 Lectures*, 62.

> biased remainder of mankind acknowledge the rectitude of his decisions and effectively abide by them?[25]

The final dead end of decline Lonergan presents in dramatic statement: "So we are brought to the profound disillusionment of modern man and to the focal point of his horror. He had hoped through knowledge to ensure a development that was always progress and never decline. He has discovered that the advance of human knowledge is ambivalent, that it places in man's hands stupendous power without necessarily adding proportionate wisdom and virtue, that the fact of advance and the evidence of power are not guarantees of truth, that myth is the permanent alternative to mystery and mystery is what his hubris rejected."[26]

The Solution

If progress is mated with decline, if the insight of creative intelligence is matched within human history by the flight from understanding and the refusal of insight, then the answer will be some higher viewpoint within human knowing. The biases of the individual and the group create short-term decline, but the bias of common sense itself creates a longer cycle of decline. This "longer cycle is to be met, not by any idea or set of ideas on the level of technology, economics, or politics, but only by the attainment of a higher viewpoint in man's understanding and making of man."[27]

More fully, what is needed is a new science of man, one which is empirical, dealing with man and the human situation as in fact they are found to be, and yet one which is critical, able to discern within the concrete situation insight and bias, progress and decline.[28] Further, the norms by which this new science issues its critique will be those of intelligence itself; for progress flows from insight and decline from the refusal of insight. The concrete norm of the new empirical and critical human science will be the intelligent and reasonable itself. "But the social situation is

25. Lonergan, *Insight*, 690. The reference in this quotation to minds and wills occasions a note. While the analysis here has been exclusively in terms of intelligence—the dominant emphasis of Lonergan, especially in *Insight*—there is in fact a parallel analysis in terms of will. Then technology becomes the "good of order," and man's predicament a "moral impotence." But detailing this would exceed the scope of the present study.

26. Lonergan, *Insight*, 549.

27. Lonergan, *Insight*, 233.

28. Lonergan, *Insight*, 235–236.

the cumulative product of individual and group decisions, and as these decisions depart from the demands of intelligence and reasonableness, so the social situation becomes, like the complex number, a compound of the rational and irrational. Then if it is to be understood, it must be met by a parallel compound of direct and inverse insights, of direct insights that grasp its intelligibility and of inverse insights that grasp its lack of intelligibility."[29]

Not force, then, but detached intelligence—detached in the sense of unbiased—is the answer to the human predicament. "The general bias of common sense has to be counterbalanced by a representative of detached intelligence that both appreciates and criticizes, that identifies the good neither with the new nor with the old, that, above all else, neither will be forced into an ivory tower of ineffectualness by the social surd nor, on the other hand, will capitulate to its absurdity."[30]

The question, however, is whether such a higher viewpoint is within man's power. It is obviously beyond the abilities of common sense, because common sense is afflicted with a bias that will dog its each new application; it is simply unable by its nature to envision the long-term good in its theoretical implications. Further, even if it could, by an impossible supposition, grasp the secret of true and long-term practicality, there would still exist a failure of will. Concern for the future requires a high moral attainment, possessed only by a few.[31] "Finally, practical people are guided by common sense. They are immersed in the particular and concrete. They have little grasp of large movements or of long-term trends. They are anything but ready to sacrifice immediate advantage for the enormously greater good of society in two or three decades."[32]

The obvious alternative to common sense, in searching for such a critical science of man, would be to appeal to philosophy. But even philosophy may be tainted. Philosophers quite as much as men of common sense are subject to the flight from understanding as well as the achievement of insight. The turn to philosophy does not ensure an escape from the dialectic of the human situation, for a philosophy may rest its case upon the surd within human affairs instead of upon the intelligence and reasonableness of unbiased intelligence. More often, perhaps, it will itself

29. Lonergan, *Insight*, 628–629.

30. Lonergan, *Insight*, 237.

31. Lonergan, *Second Collection*, 115–16.

32. Lonergan, *Method in Theology*, 360–61.

represent some incoherent mixture of the two.[33] Further, even were philosophy to attain a viewpoint and a position utterly true to the demands of creative intelligence, a host of practical problems would remain.

> The objective situation is all fact, but partly it is the product of intelligence and reasonableness and partly it is the product of aberration from them. The whole of man is all fact, but it also is malleable, polymorphic fact. No doubt, a subtle and protracted analysis can bring to light the components in that polymorphic fact and proceed to a dialectical criticism of any proposal or programme. But to whom does it bring the light? To how many? How clearly and how effectively? Are philosophers to be kings or kings to learn philosophy? Are they to rule in the name of wisdom subjects judged incapable of wisdom? Are all the members of our democracies to be philosophers? Is there to be a provisional dictatorship while they are learning philosophy?[34]

The incapacity for sustained development characteristic of common sense is thus, in the final analysis, the inability of man himself, as such. If the bias of common sense renders it incompetent to deal with the issue of decline, "on a deeper level it makes manifest the inadequacy of man." For the overcoming of the long-term cycle of decline "is conditioned by the possibility of a critical human science, and a critical human science is conditioned by the possibility of a correct and accepted philosophy."[35]

What Lonergan' s analysis suggests, accordingly, is that a realistic humanism will have to look beyond itself and seek resources other than its own. Such a solution will be, in other words, "super-natural." "The humanist viewpoint loses its primacy, not by some extrinsicist invasion, but by submitting to its own immanent necessities. For if the humanist is to stand by the exigencies of his own unrestricted desire, if he is to yield to the demands for openness set by every further question, then he will discover the limitations that imply man's incapacity for sustained development, he will acknowledge and consent to the one solution that exists and, if that solution is supernatural, his very humanism will lead beyond itself."[36]

Naturally, this appeal of reason beyond reason will be anathema to a rationalism that prides itself on leaving behind the obscurancies of the

33. Lonergan, *Insight*, 690–691.

34. Lonergan, *Insight*, 630.

35. Lonergan, *Insight*, 690.

36. Lonergan, *Insight*, 728.

past to bask in the light of modern consciousness. But Lonergan is not without his own counter-critique of the Enlightenment. "Human knowledge results from a vast collaboration of many peoples over uncounted millennia. The necessary condition of that collaboration is belief. What any of us knows, only slightly results from personal experience, personal discovery, personally conducted verification; for the most part it results from believing. But the eighteenth-century Enlightenment was not content to attack religious belief. It prided itself on its philosophers. It set up a rationalist individualism that asked people to prove their assumptions or else regard them as arbitrary. In effect it was out to destroy not only the religious tradition but all tradition."[37]

The solution to man's penchant for decline, in other words, demands a shift from a philosophical to a theological framework. Then the surd in the human situation is seen as, in fact, sin. "There is a theological dimension that must be added to our detached analysis of the compounding of man's progress with man's decline. Bad will is not merely the inconsistency of rational, self-consciousness; it is also sin against God. The hopeless tangle of the social surd, of the impotence of common sense, of the endlessly multiplied philosophies, is not merely a cul-de-sac for human progress; it also is reign of sin, a despotism of darkness; and men are its slaves."[38]

Similarly, if the inability to cope with the long-term cycle of decline reveals the basic inadequacy of man, then the answer to the human predicament is to be sought not first of all in man's initiative, but in God's. A human science, to put it in other terms, can be fully concrete and realistic if it recognizes sin within the human situation precisely as sin and then looks to God for forgiveness and re-integration. Indeed, if God is offering a solution to man's plight, and humanity disdains the solution, then its best efforts will only make the situation worse.

> For an adequate understanding reveals the manner in which man can remedy the evil in his situation. But the solution to man's problem of evil has been seen to lie, not in a human initiative, but in an acceptance of the solution God has provided; and while empirical human science can lead on to the further context of the solution, the systematic treatment of the solution itself is theological. In a word, empirical human science can become practical only through theology, and the relentless

37. Lonergan, *Second Collection*, 185.

38. Lonergan, *Insight*, 692.

> modern drift to social engineering and totalitarian controls is the fruit of man's effort to make human science practical though he prescinds from God and from the solution God provides for man's problem.[39]

The higher viewpoint by which man can overcome the bias of common sense and the long-term cycle of decline will be some kind of faith, by which God shares with human beings something of his own higher vision and thus takes them into collaboration with himself in providing a solution to their predicament. Consequently, the theological virtues are not of a purely private religious interest but have immediate and deep implications for the welfare and the survival of the human race.

> The supernatural virtues of faith, hope and charity are named theological because they orientate man to God as he is in himself. None the less they possess a profound social significance. Against the perpetuation of explosive tensions that would result from the strict application of retributive justice, there is the power of charity to wipe out old grievances and make a fresh start possible. Against the economic determinism that would result were egoistic practicality given free rein, there is the liberating power of hope that seeks first the kingdom of God. Against the dialectic discernible in the history of philosophy and the development-and-decline of civil and cultural communities, there is the liberation of human reason through divine faith.[40]

Conclusion

A review of the movement of Lonergan' s thought is necessary here. It begins with technology, which it presents by emphasizing in it the presence of intelligence at work: the insight of the inventor, the realized idea of the technical product, the know-how of the technician, the capable common sense of the manager and the entrepreneur. Such insight is not static but turns a wheel of progress; the new technical products tend to create a better situation, giving rise to new ideas, new inventions, better organization and systems of delivery. Such progress is not difficult to discern empirically when the upward curve of technological triumph in recent human history is even briefly considered.

39. Lonergan, *Insight*, 745.

40. Lonergan, *Collection*, 118.

But the story of intelligence on the march has also its darker side. Insight is accompanied by a flight from understanding; the reasonableness of creative intelligence is sacrificed to other, less worthy motives. Individual and group bias distort the unfolding of the pure desire to know and create inept and incoherent policies. Most destructively, common sense as such has a built-in bias toward short-term results and immediate practical applications, without viewing objectively the long-term and ultimate consequences. The resulting surd is incarnated into the social situation itself, thus providing poor ground for conceiving future inventions and social policies and structures. The momentum of flight from insight feeds on itself to produce a dead end of decline. Nor is such a bias toward short-term considerations difficult to discern empirically. Love Canal, for example, and the huge problem of waste cleanup it symbolizes, bears mute testimony to an exploitation of the present with scarce regard for the future.

The inability of common sense to orientate itself toward the ultimate, theoretical and long-term issues evokes an appeal to philosophy; but philosophy itself is no surer guide because it possesses no guarantee of escape from the pernicious effects of bias and the human surd. The only solution to the cognitional inadequacy of man, Lonergan concludes, is an openness to a still higher viewpoint: which includes not only man and nature, but God as well, which conceives the surd as sin, the desired solution as an initiative of God, which envisions the liberation of reason through faith, and the answer to man's problem as a collaboration with God in effecting the proferred solution.

Bibliography

Koyré. Alexandre. «Dur Monde de l'à peu près a l'Univers de la Precision," 806–823

Lonergan, Bernard. SJ. *Bernard Lonergan: 3 Lectures*. Montreal: Thomas More Institute for Adult Education, 1975. *Collection: Papers by Bernard Lonergan*. Edited by F. Crowe. New York: Herder & Herder, 1967.

———. *Insight: A Study of Human Understanding*. Revised students' edition. New York: Philosophical Library, 1958.

———. *Method in Theology*. New York: Herder & Herder, 1972.

———. "The Ongoing Genesis of Methods." *Studies in Religion/Sciences Religieuses* 6, no. 4 (1976–1977) 341–355.

———. *Philosophy of God, and Theology*. Philadelphia: Westminster Press, 1973.

———. *A Second Collection*. Edited by W. Ryan and B. Tyrrell. Philadelphia: Westminster Press, 1974.

———. *Verbum: Word and Idea in Aquinas*. Edited by David Burrell. Notre Dame: University of Notre Dame Press, 1967.

Essay 5

The Believer in the Presence of Technique[1]

André Malet

Translated by Jim Grote

1.

The believer in the presence of technique naturally implies the believer in the presence of science. In fact, in what follows we will see the extent to which one cannot speak of one without the other. To begin let us listen to some verses written in the 18th century, while noting that the "Learned Sisters" in question are not the Muses of traditional poetry, but mechanics, geometry, chemistry, that is to say, the sciences.

> Learned Sisters, faithful be
> to what my verses can foresee.
> Through the arts are going to unfurl
> a hundred new beauties across the world.
> By the efforts that you have in store
> our days will soon be lengthened more
> than those that were once so quickly ended.
> And already, on the darkened shore transcendent
> Atropos pays us less attention
> while Lachesis spins us an addition.[2]

1. Translated from Malet, "Le Croyant en face de la technique," 417–430, slightly revised.

2. de la Motte, "L'Academi des Sciences," 95–99.

The poet, who wrote these verses in an ode on the Academy of Sciences, is Antoine Houdar de la Motte (1672-1731), a friend of Fontenelle and the scholars of the age, and a determined partisan of the Moderns against the Ancients. His text provides an accurate intuition of the essence of science and technique. Science and technique do not appear here as one of the degrees of an ordered hierarchy or as one of the realms of a given domain, but already as an ensemble, as a "world" in the sense that modern thought has given or perhaps in part restored to this word. Science and technique are not only as vast as the world, but above all they confer on it another appearance, referred to by Houdar as the "hundred new beauties" leading from one world to another. This transformation has, at least in part, a human origin: the anthropological character of science and technique is seen not only in the fortunate effects that they bestow on men—"Atropos pays us less attention"—but also in their source itself, because our author does not doubt the decisive role played by man in the birth of mechanics, algebra, anatomy, and chemistry. At the same time, however, in a sincere sentiment, he speaks of this birth as of an advent which surpasses the simple human possibilities. In fact he addresses the "learned Sisters" which he respects, as if they were beings independent of man: it is "through you," he says to them; it is "by the efforts that you have in store" that the fate of mortals will be changed. There is more than a metaphor or a poetic turn of phrase here, and besides a poetic phrase is always more than a poetic phrase.

Science and technique are in fact a unifying and totalizing project. Unifying because this project produces a synthesis from the fundamental perspectives which constitute it, totalizing because this synthesis extends to the ensemble of the real disclosed under a certain aspect. A "world" is possible only to the extent that there is a unified reduction of all the manifestations of being within the realm of a given meaning. It suffices to say that this unity is not a subjective unity, imposed after the fact on heterogeneous elements and consequently external to the terms that it reunites. The unifying project does not operate from the outside: on the contrary it is through it that what is gathered together is disclosed. The unity is a horizon, that which is present to each thing. In order for each thing to become manifest it must conform to the global signification that constitutes the very essence of the project, so that it is in and by their very arising that the phenomena are unified.

The synthesis is thus not subsequent but antecedent to its contents. It is not a mathematical summation; it is, if not the source, at least the occasion for the appearance of phenomena, the ground against which they stand out and out of which they are revealed, discovering their own essence and entering into a determined pattern of relations. It is being itself which is disclosed under a certain mode and as a certain sphere which imposes itself on human liberty, having an entirely reflexive attitude on its part. The reflexive attitude intervenes only afterwards; it is the simple capture of consciousness from what is given to one's freedom as an invitation that it can only outwardly decline. The project is thus a determined disclosure of the real but grounded in the mode of appearance corresponding to the real itself.

It is not sufficient to say that science and technique constitute a project. If, in fact, science and technique are closely connected (as the history of the last three centuries, and with even more lucidity the contemporary age, confirms), it is still the case that they are not expressed by a project identical at all points. Let us begin therefore by analyzing the scientific project and saying immediately that in science the real is disclosed as object. Everything that exists is seen within the horizon of the object. What does this mean? It is necessary here to reject the illusion of many scientists, which is that of common sense. When the man on the street says, "It is objective," he believes he has arrived at reality such as it exists in itself, independent of the human subject. But he is deceived. In a general fashion, ordinary knowledge, or the kind we use in our everyday activities, is derived from a long apprenticeship by the growing child. For the child it is work to learn correctly to distinguish "objects," to call a chair a chair, a house a house, not to confuse right and left, to name the world in one word, and to name himself.

This knowledge, which for the growing child will be the very breath of his life, which is concerned with the most elementary needs of food and shelter, which serves to designate or to satisfy, whose most exalted forms are expressed in science and in culture, in short what the entire world calls the knowledge of beings and things—it is precisely this knowledge which is not the knowledge of beings and of things such as they exist in themselves. Objective knowledge perceives beings and things insofar as they are before me, understandable and knowable by me. In a most general manner, this knowledge knows the world insofar as the latter wishes to fall into its grasp; and this is why the world known in this way, but known only in this way, is an available world. This is also why man can take from the world what nourishes him, what clothes him, can build cities, lay out highways of communication, establish factories, develop agriculture, industry and economy, in a word, can live in the world and of the world.

Science not only belongs to this objectifying knowledge but is also the model achieved by it. Science is defined as "the theory of the real." This definition is accurate, but only on the condition that one carefully weighs its terms. It is not a matter of theory in the sense understood by the Greeks. The Greek *theoria*, from which the world "theory" is derived, is formed by *thea* and *orao*. The term *thea* designates the aspect under which some thing manifests itself, while *orao* signifies the attentive beholding of what is thus manifested. To this mode of knowledge corresponds a way of life: the *bios theoretikos* which is opposed to the *bios praktikos*, that is to the life of action and production. On the contrary the *bios theoretikos* designates the life of one who beholds the pure appearance of that which is present. The highest expression of this way of life is obviously thought. Greek "theory" is thus the respectful attention given to that which discloses itself, without the active, and still less the possessive, intervention of man. In the eyes of the Greeks, it constitutes the most fully realized form of human existence; it is the pure relation to the pure manifestation of the pure thing. With the Romans, *theoria* is rendered as *contemplatio*. And already, in this simple translation, the essentially practical Roman spirit is marked. In fact, *contemplatio* comes from *templum*, which is the Greek *temenos*. *Temnein* means to cut, to separate. Originally *templum*, as a separated area between sky and earth, indicated a definite region in which oracles read the future in the flight of birds, in their cries and in their manner of eating. Consequently, in the Latin *contemplatio* we find the notion of an active, incisive and separative look in which the Roman announces himself as grand jurist, grand builder, grand conqueror, grand transformer of the world. In the expression "science is the theory of the real," the word "theory"' acquires just such a significance. Modern science is that theory which stalks the real in order to obtain certainty of it. Certainly one often hears science proclaimed to be "disinterested," and that consequently, far from desiring to modify and still less elaborate the real, science, on the contrary, puts everything to work in order to know it "such as it is." But it is not necessary to be misled by this common sense illusion which we have rejected. Science knows the real only insofar as it is the objective. As Max Planck has said: "The real is what can be measured."

In speaking of measure one not only recalls the capital importance of mathematics in contemporary science and the idea of calculation in the technical sense, but one is also reminded of a more profound meaning in which "to calculate" signifies to take into consideration, to devise plans, to count with and on. Mathematics is much more than a series of operations. It tends toward total unification (as exemplified by Einstein's unified field theory) and consequently "calculates by means of" a fundamental equation. Before "calculating," mathematics "calculates by means of" scientific theory, a theory which "calculates by means of" a calculable reality. Heisenberg has said that contemporary physics aspires to "be able to write a unique fundamental equation from which proceed the properties of all the elementary particles, and from that the behavior of matter in general." Thus, in the expression "science is the theory of the real," we discern interest in a particular kind of reality, namely objectifiable being, and of a kind of theory which is not the Greek theory directed toward pure appearance, but a calculating and objectifying intention. *Science is the encounter of an objectifying look with an objectifiable reality.* Naturally the encounter is not valuable only to physics or the natural sciences; it is valuable to the human sciences as well—psychology, sociology, economics, etc. These sciences are concerned with man only insofar as he is an objectifiable being, only insofar as he is a being by means of which one can calculate and which, consequently, one can calculate. One can calculate him because one can calculate by means of him.

If science is what has just been described, the passage from theory to technique is easily understood: technique is the necessary consequence of science. It represents a farther step into the domain of the calculable and the available. The objectification is transformed here by what can be called, with Heidegger, the setting-up (*Ge-stell*). Technology sets-up being, that is to say objectifies it to the second degree, or transforms it into instrument. The remote origin of technique again rests with the Greeks. This appears to contradict what has just been said of Greek theory as the view of the pure appearance. But Greek thinking taken as a whole is ambiguous, and can also be characterized as a *techné*, technique. One could say that the development from the age of Greek philosophy to (at least half of) Western culture takes place so to speak under the patronage of the "work of art." This term designates any thing constructed by man, whether house, ship, or what today we call a work of fine art (statue, painting, etc.). The work of *techné* is an "idea" realized in a "matter" (a ship is a "form" realized in the wood, the iron, etc.). Now, it is by reference to a constructed thing that the Greeks represented "Ideas." It is also as the matter of a construction that they represented the inferior world of *hylé*, matter. Finally it is on the model of construction that they represented concrete beings (man, animal) as composed of matter and form, the ensemble of which constitutes the *kosmos*—a word derived from *kosmios*, meaning a constructed thing that is harmonious in the proportions of its constitutive matter and form. Even ethics is conceived on the model of some constructed thing. It is up to man to realize the Idea, yet he is unable immediately to do so because he also participates in the inferior world of matter. He must therefore make himself after the manner in which the craftsman or artist realizes in matter the ideal which he has conceived. Man has to "form" himself (it is remarkable that today we still speak constantly of the "formation" of body, spirit, and heart), which he is able to do by means of that virtue (*areté*) which is the same as a craftsman's ability to realize his ideal. As the work proceeds man approaches his perfection, he becomes—in the technical terms of Greek ethics—"harmonious," "well arranged," "well proportioned," "well fit," "well measured." This ethical terminology is seen to be entirely borrowed from the domain of construction and production.

However, there is a great difference between Greek *techné* and modern technique. The Greeks never went beyond the craft stage. Moreover, they applied the word "technique" to something which we consider the very opposite of technique, namely, the fine arts. This alone suffices to illustrate the abyss which separates us. Greek technique was still only a timid objectification, related more to the domain of knowing than making; it remained close to theory. By contrast, modern technique is a veritable provocation addressed to nature in order to compel it to provide the greatest possible amount of energy. In our technique there is only one thing which counts: the production and storing of energy. The peasant of old, for example, did not "torture" the earth. For him, to sow the grain was to entrust it to the natural forces of growth, and he contented himself with watching over its increase. His labor consisted more in vigilance than in action, as has been well expressed by Victor Hugo in the celebrated poem which exalts "the august gesture of the sower."[3] This was not a provoking gesture; it was a gesture of trust or confidence. Today the work of the peasant is a veritable summons addressed to the earth. Agriculture has become, or tends more and more to become, an industry. It is a matter of extracting from the soil everything it can give by working it in a multitude of ways. Fertilizers, by which the soil is made fertile, are only

3. Hugo, "Saison des Semailles," 231.

a ruse in order to destine it, in the strong sense of the word "destine," to man. Technique makes man the purpose of the world, of nature. Nature is thus determined or fixed by and for man. The character of the substratum of the earth is determined by its ability to supply minerals; the character of minerals themselves by their ability to supply, for example, uranium; uranium by its ability to supply atomic energy; atomic energy by its ability to satisfy a thousand and one ends, peaceful or destructive. What is a hydroelectric plant? It is a summons addressed to the water of the river to render up its hydraulic pressure, which is the summons addressed to the turbines to turn, which are themselves a summons addressed to the machines which anticipate electrical energy production. The hydroelectric plant is not constructed on the river in the manner of the old bridge of the Middle Ages, which joined one shore to the other. Instead, it is the river which is part of the essence of the hydroelectric plant, so that it is less a river than a source ordered toward energy.

The technical process consists of unlocking energy, transforming the energy unlocked, storing the energy transformed, distributing the energy stored, and utilizing the energy distributed. Nature is no longer simply objectified, as in theoretical science: it is compelled, ordered, or as we have just called it with Heidegger, set-up. To set-up is to stop "someone" and demand an answer. More profoundly, to set-up is to place under the rule of reason, which demands that things give an account of themselves.

However, we do not intend, as was indicated at the beginning, to expound and defend a purely anthropological conception of science and technique. It would be a mistake to think that the scientific-technical age is the exclusive product of human intelligence and will. If ancient man did not invent the automobile or the airplane, it is not because he did not desire it or desired it only hypothetically, but because "the time had not yet come." And now that it has come modern man is not free to suppress science and technique, nor even to ignore them. The most implacable of our rare contemporaries who are opposed to science and technique are nevertheless quite comfortable because of their service. The most determined "reactionaries" are the first to use modern inventions to their profit. All of this points to the fact that the technological age is less an initiative of man than a destiny which is imposed on him, less a decision of the will than a mode of appearance of being. If man provokes nature, it is because he himself is provoked to provoke it. It is the real which is manifested as a calculable and foreseeable ensemble of forces. It remains that man must respond to this summons: without this, there would be neither science nor technique. And this is why the latter are not diabolical but liberating. We have to acknowledge the danger in science and technique, but this is only the negative aspect of a positive reality and the possible obverse of a liberating call in which man is held.

It is easier now to discern the exact relationship that connects science and technique. In the historical order of discoveries, science precedes and technique follows. Modern natural science began in the 17th century. Technique properly so called did not develop before the second half of the 18th century. But in the more profound order of things, it is technique which is primary. As the Greeks held: That which is earlier in regard to its rise into dominance becomes manifest to us men only later. The order of demonstration is not the order of discovery. From the point of view of essence, the setting-up is more original. The setting-up is the motive hidden from theoretical knowledge. It is this which allows us to understand scientific objectification, which it has secretly inspired from the beginning.

This is what explains how science is a way of stalking nature, considered as a calculable ensemble of forces. One could argue, it is true, that modern physics is more and more obliged to give up the exclusively objective made of representation which it hitherto possessed. Bertrand Russell joked that electricity is not a thing like St. Paul's cathedral—which is to say that, for science, the real is a system of mathematical symbols. But this is precisely the most profound essence of objectification. Pushed to the extreme limit objectification makes the object itself disappear, leaving room for nothing but the pure subjugating grasp. Therefore, modern technique is in no way, as is often said, applied science, since it is theoretical physics itself which is technique in its deepest essence. More correctly, technique has always been the directing power for science, and, in this role, technique precedes science.

2.

We have seen that science and technique are a project which, like every project, is unifying and totalizing. We have attempted to define their nature accordingly: as a project which objectifies and which sets-up. Science-technique unifies and totalizes the real by objectifying it and by setting-it-up. But what is faith? It is also a unifying and totalizing project, but of an entirely different character; God is *par excellence* the being who cannot be objectified or set-up. To try is, properly speaking, to sin; it is to deny God as fully as one can. God reveals himself as the one who is never a being that is commanded, but always as the Lord who commands all in all and who no thing or person commands. God is the suppression, the humiliation, the crucifixion of the man of science and technique. The call that God addresses to us by his revelation in Christ is a call to despair of ourselves, of our powers, of all that we do, have, and are. It is a call which is the very antithesis of the call of science and technique. In these latter the world offers itself to objectification and the setting-up. In faith the world is disclosed as the creation of God, that is as a reality which exacts our respect and which resists all provocation and all summons on our part. In the project of faith I renounce power over the world and, like Francis of Assisi, I speak of my brother the sun and my sister the water.

The question of knowing where our true being lies thus presents itself. For it is undeniable that we need science and technique simply in order to exist. Moreover, we have seen it is not possible to reject them simply by the inclination of our will. One of our most important tasks is to respond to the call that presents the world to us in such a way that it is revealed as objectifiable and able-to-be-set-up. To refuse would be in some way to sin against this call, to sin against ourselves. Our refusal would condemn humanity to return to what it was, that is to say, condemn it to death, because life does not tolerate immobilization and still less a return to the past. Immobilization and return to the past are a fate worse than death.

Nevertheless, there is a double danger in science and technique: on the one hand, there is the forgetting of their true essence and therefore our own true essence, and on the other hand, the forgetting of other modes of the appearance of being. The mission of the man of science is to disclose the real as measurable, and thus to present the first temptation: the temptation of reducing man to the measurable, the temptation to forget that our proper essence belongs not to the measurable but to the disclosing of the measurable, the temptation to forget that we are a response to a call. By such a misjudgment we pose as lords of the earth and at the same time (ironically enough) we proceed by this very fact towards the extreme point where we will be no more than the measurable. By desiring thus to pose as the master, man becomes the slave. By desiring thus to save himself, he perishes. By conforming himself in an exclusive way to the provocation of the setting-up, he ends up no longer understanding himself as the origin of the setting-up and, in doing this, transforms himself into a thing able-to-be-set-up, if not a thing set-up. Henceforth he is a being without liberty, a being who no longer experiences anything except himself. In fact there is freedom only in the proper vocation of man, only in the truth of this vocation, which consists in the act of disclosure, that is to say in the response made to the question posed by destiny.

Suffice it to say—and here we touch on the second danger—that modern man by going to the very end of science and technique, risks taking all his standards from them. He risks coming to believe that there is only one type of a call and only one type of response, that is to say he risks, in Pascal's terms, not recognizing the difference between "orders."[4] In popularized science and in statements concerning the significance of great public events on TV, radio, or in the press, it is often repeated that the major danger of science and technique is the threat of an apocalyptic holocaust. Moreover, it is not impossible that there is here a little naiveté, demagogy, or both, on the part of opinion makers, those who can senselessly bewitch by generating obsessions. In reality, it is necessary to keep in mind what is called "the balance of terror," so that ours may be the age of the most terrible means of destruction and the most preserved from great disaster. The true danger lies elsewhere, in what we have referred to as a lack of recognition of orders. This is at the very heart of what man risks losing through peace and opulence, if not relative well-being (since opulence may not continue tomorrow). The growth and preponderance of the scientific-technical project risks concealing the existence or even worse, of altering the essence and hiding the importance of other projects, above all the humanist and religious projects, but also the economic, social, and political projects.

Objectification and setting-up threaten to conceal all other disclosures, particularly those in which pure appearance manifests itself, those in which it is not a matter of taking but of receiving. Science and technique exclude by their stamp all other disclosures, at first because of their actuality (we live in the scientific-technical age) and then by their very character (they proceed in a direction opposed to that project in which man is more servant than lord). It is clear, for example, that politics can be turned into the means *par excellence* of objectifying and of setting-up the citizens of any country, thanks to modern communication and because of the technical complexity of problems. (Still, it is necessary to

4. Cf Pascal, *Pensees*, 283 and 793.

guard against all demagogy. Was the man of the time of Ramses II, the "*ancien regime*," the Napoleonic age, or even the one immediately preceding our own, any more free than we are?)

Man can thus lose himself in science and technique. How can we ward off this danger? Is faith the only means? It is the only *radical* means because, as we have said, God is essentially the being who cannot be objectified or set-up. As he is the creator of man and of the world, man and the world can have their definitively true being only in him, as Augustine as expressed in these famous words: "For Thou hast made us for Thyself and our hearts are restless till they rest in Thee."[5] Therefore the definitive authenticity of man is found not in the scientific-technical project but in the project of faith, which considers God as the creator and the world as his creation. It is true, and we have stressed it enough, that nature lends itself to objectification and setting-up and that it even provokes man to provoke it in this way. But only in this way? Is this way the primordial and the final way? Can nature find its completion here?

Does it not aspire to something else, that something else expressed in the mysterious phrase of the Epistle to the Romans. "For the creation waits with eager longing for the revealing of the sons of God; for the creation was subjected to futility, not of its own will but by the will of him who subjected it in hope; because the creation itself will be set free from its bondage to decay and obtain the glorious liberty of the children of God. We know that the whole creation has been groaning in travail unto now" (Romans 8: 19–22). Luther's profound commentary on this passage, which one might describe as written expressly for our technical era, reads as follows:

> The philosophers so direct their gaze at the present state of things that they speculate only about what things are and what quality they have, but the apostle calls our attention away from a consideration of the present and from the essence and accidents of things and directs us to their future state. For he does not use the term "essence" or "activity" of the creature, or its "action," "inaction," and "motion," but in an entirely new and marvelous theological word he speaks of the "expectation of the creation," so that because his soul can hear the creation waiting, he no longer directs his attention to our inquiries about the creation itself, but rather to what it is awaiting . . . . Therefore you will be the best philosophers and the best explorers of the nature of

5. Augustine, *Confessions* I, i.

> things if you will learn from the apostle to consider the creation as it waits, groans, and travails, that is, as it turns away in disgust from what now is and desires that which is still in the future. For then the study of the nature of things, their accidents and their differences, will quickly grow worthless . . . . Look how we esteem the study of the essences and actions and inactions of things, and the things themselves reject and groan over their own essences and actions and inactions![6]

Thus, according to Paul and Luther, nature aspires to its deliverance. Indeed, it lends itself to objectification and to setting-up, but this is only temporary and of value here below. What the future will be, how it will manifest itself as regards regenerated nature, this disdain and lament of its actual essence of which Luther speaks, cannot be known nor even imagined, because our attempt to do so can only proceed from the assumed elements to our actual experience. The future hope would thus be only a simple transportation of the present, that is to say a pseudo-future.

What is true for the word is, *a fortiori*, true for man. His definitively true being may be mistaken to consist in the project of objectifying and setting-up which is in truth only temporarily his task. The day will come when redeemed man will be able to speak in all truth, and not only in hope, of his brother the sun and his sister the water. What is symbiosis of man and the world through God their common creator will be, we do not know. Just as strongly as Jesus and the New Testament are affirmative of the fact, to the same extent they are silent on how the fact will be manifested. The matter is all the more remarkable considering that Jews were so fond of all sorts of details about the future life, so that their apocalypses have left us the most fantastic descriptions about it. Jesus for his part always refused to give any picture of the glory to come. To the celestial bliss he applied the simple name "the Life" (*he zoe*). Since he speaks of it unceasingly, it is necessary to conclude that this fact was of capital importance to him. But since he has not given any description of it, it is necessary to conclude that how the fact will be manifested is inexpressible. To be sure he does speak once, in passing, of the new wine in the Kingdom (Mark 14:25). But is it necessary to see more than an image here? Paul, for his part, is also entirely sober. He equally renounces any portrayal of the life to come. The future, for him, is entirely and simply the "*me blepomenon*" (2 Corinthians 4:18), that which is not seen, that which is not visible. Elsewhere he is content to speak of the "glory" which

6. Luther, *Commentary on Romans*, 360–362.

will be revealed (Romans 8:18; 2 Corinthians 4:17), of the "being-with-Christ" which will begin then (1 Thessalonians 4: 17, 5:10; Philippians 1:23; 2 Corinthians 5:7–8) and of the view face to face (1 Corinthians 3:2). John is no more explicit. Eternal life is the central theme in his gospel, but this life is only affirmed. It is never described because all representation of the Kingdom to come would only be able to speak of human possibilities, and the most elevated of these would be no better than the most primitive description of the *zoe*, the promised life. What does the believer thus know concerning the future life? Simply this, that it will be the life of God. Simply this, that it will be at first the judgement and annihilation of the present life, in order to be then its fulfillment. Simply this, that the Kingdom of God is a Kingdom where the objectification and the setting-up will have no place. Simply this, that the meaning of all worldly projects will be reversed, and that it is in this reversal of meaning that the resurrection and the life consist.

But in the meantime, what is the situation of the believer? What is the conflict between faith and technique? If everything we have said up to now is correct, the conflict cannot be what we once thought it was. The problem of the relationship of science and faith appeared for a long time as a problem of limits. Particular issues were argued about because the world of faith appeared to be the only world. The believers gave in to the same temptation that threatens science, and which we have rejected: the totalitarian temptation which comprehends only one type of call and only one type of response. We quarreled therefore inside the same world. We imagined, for example, that every position regained concerning the form of the earth or its movement reinstated the world of faith. Likewise, in our days the problem of miracles is posed and resolved by many believers in an incorrect way: they conceive God's action as taking place outside natural causes, whereas in reality God's action is within natural causes, in such a way that it escapes the objectifying look. Many of those who flatter themselves on having solved the problem of miracles still more or less confuse different planes and the calls that they make. To justify their position, they sometimes appeal to the indeterminism of atomic physics as the best proof of their position.

All things considered, however, we can see that today the process of dissociating the believing project and the scientific-technical project has been achieved. The distinction of "orders" (to speak like Pascal) or the "regions of being" (to speak like Husserl and Heidegger) have attained a perfect clarity. We know today that the real is of such a richness that it is disclosed according to several modes of appearance. The unity is no longer made by subsuming a multiplicity of terms under one univocal term, following a procedure of hierarchization. No, it is necessary to speak of a multiplicity of aims or of constituent projects. There are the projects of faith, of science, of politics, of economics, etc. We have passed from the plane of objective hierarchies to that of fundamental attitudes. The phenomenon of the conflict has not been abolished because of this, but it has changed its meaning.

What is the new meaning of the conflict which concerns faith and technique? As long as he is here below, the believer must live simultaneously in the two projects: the scientific-technical project and the project of faith. He must carry out simultaneously the objectifying disclosure and the disclosure of faith. He must consider simultaneously the world as the field of his work and action, and as the creation of God. The believer, following the profound adage of reformed theology, is a dialectical being, *simul peccator, simul justus*, at once sinful and justified or righteous. The true and integral being of man is joined in two projects. The scientific-technical project is inauthentic only when it yields to the excess we have described, when it falls into the double danger of which we have spoken: of forgetting that man belongs not to the calculable but to the unfolding of the calculable, and of forgetting that beside the objectifying project there are still more essential projects whose meaning is to manifest the pure appearance of being.

Faith is the project *par excellence* of the more essential projects, and this is why it prevents the man of science and technique from becoming the prisoner of science and technique. It shows to him in the call of science and technique a call from God, which is not comprised as such in the measure where God remains constantly present. It is the source and guarantee of the authenticity, not of science and technique, but of the man of science and technique, who is lost as soon as he forgets that his vocation comes to him from God. If faith can thus save modern humanity, it is because a being who is the judge of the world is revealed in it. Faith discloses to man that he is made for something or rather for someone who infinitely surpasses him and from whom alone he can receive his definitively true being, so that the fundamental attitude of the Christian must be that of St. Paul's *hos me*: "Those who deal with the world as though they had no dealings with it" (1 Corinthians 7:31). John prescribes the same attitude as Paul: that the believer be in the world without being of the world (cf. John 17:9–19).

Therefore, it is not necessary in any way to pass through the world without stopping, by making one's escape from it. To say that faith alone assures the authenticity of the man of science and technique is not at all to say that this man would be more authentic by renouncing science and technique. To do all things under the judgement of God does not mean to do nothing. Externally and as regards the objectifying look, nothing is changed in the activity of the believer, nothing is different from other men. He has the same human nature as they do (faith does not make him an angel); like them, he cultivates his body and his mind; like them he has a family, trade, and home. He has the same field of action as they do: the world in which, like them, he works to transform things according to the economic, social, political, cultural, artistic and moral planes. The difference between the believer and the unbeliever is situated on the plane of meaning. Not that the scientific-technical project as such has a different meaning for the believer than for the unbeliever. For both of them it is a matter of an identical task: to objectify and to set-up nature. But the believer goes much farther than the unbeliever and lays the foundation of the scientific-technical project more deeply because beyond or rather at the very heart of the provocation of the world, he perceives the provocation of God. Thus, if he is a true believer—I say "if," because who can call himself a true believer?—the scientific and technical call will be even more urgent for him than for the believer. The latter gives himself with fierce ardor to different projects, because for him the world is the only homeland of man. But when one believes, then the world is more precious still. It is the creation of God, and with what respect and what ardor should one respond to his call! But we are worthless believers, and this is why the children of the world are wiser than the children of the light (Luke 16:8). This is why the latter are invited by the Gospel itself to take the former for their model. It is still true that faith, in itself far from negating the scientific-technical project, justifies it more profoundly than unbelief. Practiced under the judgement of God, the objectification and the setting-up ought to be truer and more serious than in unbelief.

This truth acquires an infinitely greater importance on the following grounds. We have said that man cannot do without science and technique for the satisfaction of his most fundamental needs, such as food, clothing, shelter, and in a more general manner, all the necessities of his earthly life. If we recall now that the essence of the Gospel is love, that the new commandment is the commandment of love, we immediately see that the believer cannot pretend to obey this commandment if he is not interested in the temporal fate of men: "I was hungry and you gave me no food, I was thirsty and you gave me no drink, I was a stranger and you did not welcome me, naked and you did not clothe me, sick and in prison and you did not visit me" (Matthew 25:42–43). Now what are science and technique if not the means of alleviating the hunger and thirst of men, of clothing them, sheltering them, healing them and assisting them, in prison and elsewhere? Can they and must they not, therefore, be one of the highest forms of the love of neighbor? Can we not grasp, still better in this perspective, all the gravity and all the seriousness of the objectification and of the setting-up of nature?

Thus, at the end of our argument we rejoin the elder Antoine Houdar de la Motte in his wonder before the salutary possibilities offered to humanity by those "learned Sisters" who render Atropos, the goddess who cuts the thread of life, more idle, and Lachesis, the goddess who weaves it, more active. However, the analysis of the project of faith that we have made obliges us to go infinitely farther than the poet. For the same Jesus who pronounced the solemn words that we have just quoted also said that man does not live by bread alone. Man is made for God, for the eternal life with the eternal God, in which there is no more hunger, thirst, prison, sickness, death, and where consequently the "learned Sisters" have nothing more to do. Man is created for a Kingdom where science and technique have no place because they would be perfectly useless there. And the highest love that the Christian can have for men is to announce the good news of this Kingdom.

Bibliography

Hugo, Victor. «Saison des Semailles." In *Les Chansons des Rues et de Bois*, 231. Paris: Libraire Internationale, 1865.

Luther, Martin. *Commentary on Romans*. Luther's Works 25. St Louis: Concordia, Malet, André. «Le Croyant en face de la technique.» *Revue d'Histoire et de Philosophie Religieuses* 55, No. 3 (1975) 417–430.

de la Motte, Antoine Houdar. «L'Academi des Sciences.» In *Oeuvres I*, 95–99. Paris: Prault, 1754.

Pascal, Blaise. *Pensées*. Edited by Léon Brunschvicg. Lutetia Edition. Paris: Classiques Français, 1949.

Essay 6

A Christian Philosophical Perspective on Technology[1]

Egbert Schuurman

Introduction

Modern technology is fraught with problems. There are tensions between the power of technology and the freedom of man. There are economic difficulties. There are issues associated with particular technologies. And all these problematical dimensions are increasing, so that the development of nuclear energy, for instance, raises dangers which have not been previously encountered, which exhibit new proportions in space and time. Man's technological innovations tend under current circumstances to be at once irreversible and negative, especially in the natural environment. Man values nature only as an area and object of human action. He is literally consuming the very foundations upon which his life is based, using up natural material and energy resources as if they were limitless. In reality, however, these resources are not his income but his property—which is to say, again, that they are limited. With an enormous, ever-growing dynamism man is approaching the limits—and this means he is beading for catastrophe. The picture is very dark if we but think of the threatening possibilities (or *im*possibilities!) of nuclear weapons.

1. An earlier version of this essay was published in a pamphlet entitled *Technology in a Christian-Philosophical Perspective*, as no. 16 in the series F2 Brochures of the Institute for the Advancement of Calvinism.

In the meantime, people all know that the solution to these problems is no longer more and better technology. What we need more than anything else is a fundamental discussion of the spiritual roots of the modern development of our culture; we need a discussion not on the level of science and technology itself but on the level of philosophy, ethics, and religion.

Such discussions are already taking place. Jacques Ellul perhaps, but especially those influenced by him, have done considerable work in this area. Although we can learn much from their contributions, their approach is not, to my mind, wholly satisfactory. Ellul and his followers tend to assert that the problems of modern technology are too heavy to bear. As Christians they think that modern technology is an autonomous, demonic power. In *The Technological Society*—but also in later books such as *The Ethics of Freedom* and *The New Demons*—Ellul seems to argue that man is not the master of technology, but its slave and its victim. Man is the victim of a universal, artificial, monistic, self-directing power.

Now it is clear to me that to approach the future of technology from this non-biblical perspective does not leave open the possibility of deliverance. I do not agree with such a position.[2] I acknowledge, however, that it is *difficult* for people to control modern technology. The *idea* that we have to do with an autonomous development arises, I think, precisely from that difficulty. Take computer technology as an example. The computer functions autonomously, and as such gives the impression of appearance of *absolute* autonomy, whereas in reality it is only *relatively* autonomous. It must be created and directed toward some use by someone. Technology is not an autonomous force. The fact that the development and direction of technology proper are guided and set by norms given to it from the outside, and the fact that it is precisely human beings who do this,

2. In the last few years—most notably in his very lucid "Nature, Technique and Artificiality," 263–283—Ellul has ceased to speak about the absolute autonomy of technology. He even argues that there is no irreparable contradiction between technique and Christianity. He makes it clear in a way I can fully agree with that it is through sin that technology as an instrument of freedom has become our slavery. There is a dialectic in technological development. Therefore, Ellul can speak of "denying fatality" and the "refusal of fatality," which gives him the opportunity to consider limits for technology. Once more I fully agree that this is a question of ethics and human responsibility. Especially when Ellul is accenting this responsibility it seems to me that he has made a shift in his thinking. Prior to 1980 he never spoke so clearly about the origin of dialectics and the possibility of responsibility as he has done since.

make it clear that technology is a dependent phenomenon. Nevertheless, the problems are great and heavy to bear.

To understand these problems better and to assure the possibility of a new, liberating perspective, we need to adopt a Christian, biblical view of history. I shall therefore begin by suggesting the basic outlines of such a view. We shall then be in a position to consider the predominant motives in science and technology (which will enable us better to understand specific problems). Afterwards I shall sketch a Christian-philosophical perspective on technology and conclude with a reflection upon the meaning of technology: upon technology as curse and blessing.

A Biblical View of History

Men themselves cannot provide a total view of history. Many people, however, especially philosophers, try to take history in their grasp and to show their power over it. Some modern thinkers propose to use science and technology to dominate history, to make the future fully subject to human ideas. We find this inspiration and motivation on a grand scale in Marxism and modern "systems" philosophy. Yet the outcome of such an intention is inevitably the reverse of what is promised. Man becomes not the master of history, but its slave. The reason is that despite his presumed autonomy, man cannot really secure his own mastery. Mortal man cannot lord it over history. He himself is fully historical. His pretension to give meaning to history must therefore result finally in historicism, relativism, and even nihilism. And in the meantime—as in our time—science and technology manifest themselves as apparently autonomous cultural powers.

This development arises from the secularization of the Christian idea of history, a secularization which begins with man himself, his idea of autonomy, and leads to his being confronted with apparently autonomous powers. My objection to some of those influenced by Ellul is that they begin with the autonomous powers and neglect the roots: the idea of the autonomy of man. In relation to the questions of history and of human freedom and responsibility, they are therefore struggling with an incorrectly formulated problem.

According to God's revelation, man cannot speak either the first or the last word on history. He is not the giver of the meaning of history, is not autonomous, not self-sufficient, and not sovereign. To know the meaning of history, we have to acknowledge that light must come from outside history. In that light man knows by faith the meaning of history. And it is the revelation of God that places man in that light. Neither human reason nor human technology can provide such light. In the Christian perspective the corner-stone of history is not man, but the revealed Word of God in Jesus Christ. Christ is the light of the world. If man pretends to give light in history by his reason or his technology, in reality all becomes more dark. This is witnessed to even by the experience which Neo-Marxist thinkers such as Theodor Adorno and Max Horkheimer have had with the "*dialectic of enlightenment*."

What, then, is the *content* of the biblical light for an understanding of history, and of human technology within history? The Bible gives us the basics. To claim to have the basics does not mean that Christians can answer all questions. Christians can provide a biblical perspective but cannot solve all problems and difficulties. The deepest meaning of history is a divine mystery (see Deuteronomy 29:29 and Revelation 10:4). This mystery stresses, on the one hand, that man is not the master of history; but, on the other, that he is responsible for the development of history, and of culture within that history. Men are responsible for their actions, because they are servants of God and not their own masters. Let us thus examine four basic biblical givens.

1. *The cultural mandate.*

One basic biblical given is the cultural mandate for man (Genesis 1:28). Man has received the calling to dress or to build the creation, and to keep it (Genesis 2:15). Having been created in the image of God, man must work in the Kingdom of God so that everything in the creation will unfold and find its proper place. This gives man the ability to develop creation in such a responsible way that his cultural work may praise and glorify the creator, the Lord of heaven and earth (Psalm 148). It is via man's cultural task in history that the fulfillment of all possibilities in the creation is to be realized.

2. *The fall.*

A second biblical given is the fall of man from community with his creator. Man forsook his original task. He himself wanted to be God the creator. After the fall, although it remained man's task to develop culture, he could no longer fulfill the cultural mandate. History ceased to be wholesome and became instead disastrous. A way of life was changed into a way of death. What was meant to be a disclosure of creation became a distortion. The wholeness of history was broken; nature was cursed and became a threatening environment for man; man became mortal. The sin of Adam and Eve incurred a lessening of the earth's spontaneous abundance (Genesis 3); the ground refused to give her strength to the sinner Cain (Genesis 4). Sin always involves a loss of "earth" in some sense: alienation from God and alienation from creation go hand in hand.

Since the fall, history has ceased to be the unfolding of creation through the fulfillment of man's cultural task. On the contrary, history has been running ever more aground. Of this the flood, the building of a Babel culture, and the biblical history of Israel are clear manifestations. Nor can man himself restore history. Rather, he is the cause of its many dislocations and destructions. Skills and techniques of all kinds may be admirable, but the tyrannical or greedy use of human power over nature is a failure deriving from human sin, not from God's intention in the creation.

3. *Redemption.*

A third biblical given is the promise of Genesis 3:15 as fulfilled in Jesus Christ. God himself provides redemption. Jesus Christ is the second Adam. He has done what the first Adam was supposed to do and provided for the reconciliation of all things. In him the redemption and the fulfillment of creation are assured. He has all power over history to bring about the Kingdom of God (see Hebrews 2:14b, Galatians 4:4, 1 Corinthians 15:20-28). The destructive power of Satan is broken; that power is still manifest, of course, but destruction is no longer the final word. In Jesus Christ the Kingdom of God has come and is coming.

Although this perspective of the Kingdom of God now dominates history, we nevertheless continue to see and to experience dislocation, destruction, and death. Yet behind this development, as we know in faith, is the working, saving power of Jesus Christ. Through him history is placed under the sign of a total recreation, the full revelation of the Kingdom of God. Christ gathers together all things in heaven and on earth (see Ephesians 1:10, Colossians 1:15-23). At last, creation will be completed in a new heaven and a new earth. Then alienation, not only between man and God and between man and man, but also between man and animal, between man and nature, between man and technology, will come to an end (see Isaiah 11 and Revelation 21).

This perspective on history places people in expectation and gives them hope. In this perspective man can once again carry out his cultural mandate in obedience to Jesus Christ, as his follower and guided by his spirit. He is on the way to the Kingdom of God. Signs of that Kingdom are already manifest, if but darkly, here and now.

4. *Disobedience and secularization.*

The first basic given, the cultural mandate, is extended in the third, redemption. The second, the fall, is extended in the fourth, disobedience and secularization. For it is clear that not everyone lives within the dynamic power of the creation, which is in Christ the power of the Kingdom of God. Many people do not seek the Kingdom; in fact, even many deeds of Christians are not in harmony with the Kingdom of God. But for all that, people cannot escape the dynamic power of this Kingdom. It is true that instead of seeking it, they seek themselves. It is true that they take the third basic given (the Kingdom of God) and secularize it again and again in seeking the kingdom of man. Yet even when people do not accept, or do not accept any longer, the way of escape and salvation in Jesus Christ, they still cannot make themselves free from this prevailing power in history; no, they become parasites on this power. Especially in Western culture do people want to go their own way. And as they attempt to do so, the fourth feature intensifies (especially through the possibilities of modern technology) the characteristics of the fall in an expansion of chaotic, destructive, and demonic powers. Modern secularization is a particularly destructive working-out or expression of the fall.

It would be a mistake, however—and it seems to me that Ellul runs the danger of making this mistake—to conclude that the fourth line is the decisive line of history. In reality this is only a perversion of the meaning of history, a perversion which, because of the power of modern technology and its destructive effects, appears overwhelming in our time. Yet even in its most monstrous manifestations the kingdom of man is only a perverse imitation of the Kingdom of God. And it is a constant consolation to know that man on his own and by himself cannot make the meaning of creation, the Kingdom of God, impossible. On the contrary, the fact that the Kingdom of God is already on the way means that at any moment people may be converted and led once again to seek the Kingdom—even in a technological society.

It is not easy to grasp the relation of redemption and secularization, because while everything is related to the Kingdom of God, this relationship is not always a positive one. All we can say is that the fourth line will be judged by the third: redemption will triumph over disobedience; salvation will triumph over secularization. The divine mystery of history is manifest in this interrelation.

The Spiritual Roots of Modern Western Culture

The modern development of Western culture throws special light on the problem of the interrelation of secularization and redemption. Generally speaking, the Reformation led people to accept their divine calling to develop the creation. But from its beginning, the Reformation was confronted with Renaissance humanism, especially among philosophers and scientists. Since the Enlightenment of the eighteenth century, the influence of humanism has dominated. It is here that the secularization of Western culture begins. Christian eschatology is increasingly secularized and transformed into an expectation of a technological salvation. More and more, man is convinced that he can make a new world, a paradise on earth. The promise of the Gospel will be realized by man himself. Such is the secular faith. Issuing from Western culture, this secular faith in progress through science and technology, in combination with politics and economics, has flooded over the whole world. Marxism and American pragmatism are—notwithstanding differences in their political-economic systems—equally good examples of this faith.

However, the actual situation of the Western welfare state with its large-scale threat of destruction and its attendant problems makes it clear that this, too, is a way that leads to death. Never before were the cultural problems so huge and threatening as in our time; and never before has the influence of secularized expectation been so deeply rooted. Man expects salvation through technology while its opposite, destruction through technology, comes upon him. Technological society was expected to be wholesome, but has turned out to be pernicious—a monstrous, demonic order. Yet the direction in which people seek the solution to their problems is, once again, a direction characterized by science and technology. The spiritual roots do not change.

Many Christians (following Ellul) have concluded that the actual cultural situation is fully demonic and that they should therefore seek to transcend culture in order to rediscover their freedom. "Does the Bible not even teach that technology is an evil human power?" they ask. The building of the tower of Babel is commonly cited. In Genesis 11 God says, "And this they began to do and now nothing will be restrained from them which they have imagined to do." As we know, God put a stop to that aspiration for limitless power and mastery. The fact that technology first developed in the line of Cain easily leads to the conclusion that technology is in itself sinful and bad.

However, we should not overlook another important revelation in the Bible. Too often it is forgotten that in the Bible technology, as in the building of Noah's ark, is a sign of salvation. The Bible teaches that God himself gives wisdom and insight to man for technology. Exodus 35:30–35 says that Bezalel and Oholiab could not ply their technical craft without the spirit of God to inspire them.

The idea that there can be no Christian perspective for modern, technological culture is true only to the extent that it *seems* there is no way out. Even if man were to accept his responsibility, it would be difficult at present to change the massive, dynamic structures of the modern development. Their influence can only be a destructive one for a long time to come—even if people were to be converted this very day to seeking the Kingdom of God in science and technology.

Nevertheless, these sad facts will not have the last word; we have to judge the present state of affairs in culture in light of the biblical view of history. People cannot undo the power of Jesus Christ; they cannot undo the restored meaning of creation. They may well deny this power and meaning. But it may well be that the menacing problems of the secularized society are even signs of the second coming of Jesus Christ, signs of a full re-creation. "We know that the whole creation has been groaning in travail together until now." "For the creation waits with eager longing for the revealing of the sons of God" (Romans 8:22 and 19).

But what is the immediate relevance of the Christian view of history for technological development? Before dealing with this question, it is necessary to say something about the structure and history of technology, and about the dominant motives operating in modern technology.

The Structure and History of Technology

Briefly "technology" refers to the human use of tools to give form to nature for human purposes. Man's present tools have become exceptionally refined and taken over many of his functions, which have themselves multiplied. In the gigantic and dynamic technological development of modern times, the position of the tool has become one of increasing independence. Following a tool technology (think of the hammer) and an energy technology (think of the steam-engine) we are now in the stage of information technology (think of the computer). More often than not, technology today implies an enhancing of this last possibility, and is characterized by automation.[3]

The latest stage of technology is attended by many problems. We have pollution as a result of the industrial application of technology, and unemployment as a result of automation. Because of the influence of science, technological society itself takes on the spiritual characteristics of *abstractness, universality, logical rigor,* and *durability*. The complex interrelation of techniques, technological products, and systems of technology has become an apparently omnivorous, independent force that shapes and molds human life. Modern technology seems to obey its own laws, and the impression arises that it is virtually beyond control.

In such a situation many anti-technologists, and some Christians, think that we must turn away from technology. Anti-technologists say that we must return to the past. Many Christians think that their only work in the technological culture should be to witness to the coming Kingdom of Jesus Christ. But this valid and essential witness should not be allowed to become separated from the work to be done in technology itself. Otherwise, the Christian will find himself having to work on two levels at once. On the ground floor he will be working in technology itself, but on the second (and only on the second) he will be witnessing. There will be no integration between Christian faith and technology, and any opportunity to re-direct and to reform the modern culture and technology along with science, politics, and economics is precluded from the outset.

Technology is not bad in itself. The question whether we shall have to deal with the blessing of technology or with its curse will always depend on man's motivation in technology. So the primary question confronting

3. This summarizes part of a longer analysis which can be found in Schuurman, *Technology and the Future.*

us today is: What motive or motives are in fact guiding modern man in the development of technology? If a primary motive can be identified and the cause of the wrong development of technology illuminated, then a further question arises: What is the motive which ought to re-direct modern technology? And, after that, what might be the real consequences of this alternative motive?

Motives in the Development of Technology

A first or most obvious motive operative in technology is the service of economic power. When these powers dominate the development of technology, the profit-principle is absolutized. The goal becomes economic and material growth, with its concomitant emphasis on the acquisition and consumption of material goods. Under the influence of "economism" technological development becomes a rapacious force that leaves in its wake destruction and pollution, while it generates technological products that are redundant, superfluous, and even too cheap (since not all human and environmental costs are taken into account in price determination). What we typically find is a tremendous overdevelopment of the technical and economical aspects of social institutions (the gigantic scale for instance), in conjunction with an underdevelopment of other aspects. Among these are human freedom and responsibility in work, variety in economic and technical scale, stability, the aesthetic relation between technology and nature, social justice, fair relations with the Third World, and so on. All those features which might undermine strictly economic and material well-being are ignored.

A second motive operative in contemporary technology is faith in science and pursuit of its application. Indeed, the predominant character of modern science only becomes clear in technological rationalism. The result, particularly at the level of design, is a scientific technology which greatly diminishes human creativity and responsibility.

Creativity seeks expression in invention, and responsibility implies possibilities for re-direction and reformation. So absolutizing the scientific base of modern technology restricts man's liberty in shaping technology. The bent of scientific knowledge toward continuity (since it is knowledge of a fixed and determinate subject-matter) is projected into technology, which in turn becomes fixed and determinate as well.[4]

4. This again repeats an argument given at greater length in *Technology and the*

A third motive operative in contemporary technology is simply one of technology for its own sake. Let us call it the imperative to technological perfection. Many engineers are so stimulated by this motive that they feel like whatever can be made and perfected must be made and perfected. Things must always be made bigger and better. This motive leads to unchecked and aimless technological power, which engineers pretend to control and master but which in fact victimizes them. They are under the spell of their own works, and the results are the opposite of what they intend. Technology gains absolute dominance over man. Even nature and culture are threatened by this absolutized technology.

The three motives I have briefly described dominate those who are actively engaged in managing the development and social direction of technology. We come now, however, to the question of a possible basis of these motives. It is possible that the large-scale problems, issuing from modern large-scale technology have arisen because the motives involved are based on man's large-scale pretensions? Are these various motives not always related to man himself, and does this not perhaps imply a human pretension to be the center of reality?

To answer such questions, we must turn again to the spiritual history of the West. At the basis of man's scientific and technological aspirations is the idea of autonomy, of man as his own measure. The prevailing *philosophy* in Western culture originates from this idea and strives to confirm it. Philosophy thus serves a religious function. Following the Enlightenment, philosophy oriented itself to *science*, especially to natural scientific methodology. Scientism, faith in science or an absolutizing of instrumental reason, increasingly assumes the role of religion in Western culture. Modern philosophy is the bridge linking the idea of autonomy to science and its methodology. Philosophy is used to provide assurance and confidence—in a tacit, religious, devotion to the scientific-technological method as a means to master practical affairs, from engineering to economics and politics. At the basis of modern technology lies the will to power.

The Old Motive as a New One

If the direction of culture is to be one of deliverance and unfolding, the basic motive of man will have to be altered. The new motive which is

---

Future, especially page 22 and following.

required is in fact a very old one—one in which man is not the center of reality, not autonomous. It is the motive which arises from the fact that man is created in the image of God. Such a motive places responsibility on man and is expressed in the love of God and the love of one's neighbor. More particularly, in politics the will to power gives way to an institutionalization of the pursuit of justice; in economics, an absolutized profit-principle is replaced by responsible stewardship; and in science, knowledge for power is superseded by knowledge in the service of wisdom. We have to see clearly that science—and the same can be said of technology—*can* be a good servant. We have to see clearly that it is the influence and guidance of wrong motives that have made science and technology bad masters.

In relation to technology, we also need not reject the scientific basis of modern technology. I am opposed here only to the faith in autonomy that has been associated with science and technology. Science has been singled out by an apostate faith as the only road in the whole field of knowledge and action, while in fact it ought to be considered as neither more nor less than one of the pathways.

We can get a better understanding of the proper service-function of science in technology if we take note of the original motive that was called upon to inspire man in technology. The biblical motivating force in human history is the task of dressing and building, keeping and preserving creation. On the one hand, to limit the motive to "preservation" alone would imply a choice for nature and against culture; this would entail a choice of natural catastrophe, the willing of fate. On the other, to confine man to "building" alone would imply a presumptuousness neglect to consider and weigh what is wise and essential and what is not. It would be to choose cultural upheaval. Both nature and man would be threatened by nearly autonomous and destructive technological power.

However, within the twofold harmonious calling—to build and to preserve, to dress and to keep, to progress and to conserve—man, the image-bearer of God, is called to a twofold service of love. In building and at the same time preserving creation, he both confirms his love towards his creator and redeemer and at the same time lovingly represents all creation. This means, among other things, that man is responsible for the unfolding of the meaning of creation in dressing and keeping it, and at the same time that he must resist every attempt to disturb, disintegrate, and destroy this meaning—including those attempts which lead to the tremendous problems of the scientific-technological culture of our day.

Guided by the right motive, man in his cultural activity can be a blessing for nature (1 Kings 4:33–34) and at the same time enter into an open way toward the future.

The Meaning of Technology

To seek both "cultivation" and "preservation" in technology is to pour new and profound content into the high moral purposes of scientists and engineers. For it means that they should no longer arbitrarily follow their own will. Instead, they should eagerly seek to be of service in the unfolding, deepening, and enriching of the meaning of technology within the meaning of creation. Technology, since it is but a part of man's activity, can be properly evaluated only if it is set in the context of the total reality and good of man, and not judged as a self-sufficient whole exclusively in terms of its own inner laws and dynamics.[5] The purposes, values, and norms of technology should be made explicit in an ethics of technology developed on the foundations of this new ethos.

Moreover, if the prospective engineer would only realize who he is—namely, a human being marked by short-sightedness, imperfections, and a tendency to underestimate the unfavorable side-effects of his work—he could no longer be tempted to dominate technological development presumptuously, nor would he aspire to unlimited, megalomaniacal achievements. Instead, he would practice wisdom, level-headedness, carefulness, prudence, patience, modesty, and scrupulousness. He would also be prepared to subject his work continuously to critique and skepticism, to interact with his peers in order to define and accept communal responsibility. By emphasizing the responsibility of the engineers in such a way, we would be able to slow down current technological development with its ironclad logic, its gigantic dimensions and dangers, and we would be able to give attention to those areas of our cultural life which are now suffering from underdevelopment. If the engineer would do his work *coram Deo*, "before the face of God," he would be able to disclose the meaning and the blessing of technology.

Although no one could possibly supply a statement of the full richness and manifold meaning of technology, we can nevertheless express it in part. Technology is able to alleviate man's fate as forced on him "by nature." Technology can offer greater opportunities for living. It can

5. Cf. Clarke, "Technology and Man," 247–258.

reduce the physical burdens and strains inherent in labor. It can diminish the drudgery of routine duties, release the working animal, avert natural catastrophes, conquer diseases, supply homes and food, augment social security, expand possibilities for communications, increase information, enhance responsibility, advance material welfare in harmony with spiritual well-being, and help unfold the abundant qualities of individuals and nations. Moreover, technology provides time for rest and reflection, and makes room for creative leisure. It promotes new possibilities in the fields of science and technology themselves, and thus clears the way for a varied development of culture in harmony with nature. Technology also helps make possible work that is more meaningful in character. In addition to facilitating productive labor, technology creates room for work that consists in the giving of aid and service, of love and care.

Let me conclude by presenting technology as a pilgrimage of obedience, a mandated way to greater insight into the meaning of creation as the Kingdom of God. We are called upon to honor the Lord in technology as in every sphere of life. Is it not time, then, that the proclamation of a Kingdom approach to technology be made an integral component of our evangelical witness to modern, technological society?

Bibliography

Clarke, W. Norris. "Technology and Man: A Christian View." In *Philosophy and Technology Readings in the Philosophical Problems of Technology*, edited by Carl Mitcham and Robert Mackey, 247–258. New York: The Free Press, 1972.

Ellul, Jacques. "Nature, Technique and Artificiality." *Research in Philosophy and Technology* 3 (1980) 263–283.

Schuurman, Egbert. *Technology in a Christian-Philosophical Perspective*. Transvaal, South Africa: Potchefstroom University, 1980.

———. *Technology and the Future: A Philosophical Challenge* (Toronto: Wedge, 1980).

Essay 7

Christ and Technology in Dialogical Relation

Some reflections on the Technological Augmentation of the Sacred[1]

Levi Checketts

Introduction: Beyond the Five Types

H. Richard Niebuhr's five "typologies" of Christians relating to culture, we have seen, provide a useful framework for considering Christian relation to technology. Whether technology is seen as an important way of carrying out Christian discipleship, as Fudpucker contends, or antithetical to the praxis of Christian life, as Blair argues, or an utterly separate phenomenon, as Malet articulates, are important foundational considerations for a robust theological study of technology. And given that the field of theological studies of technology has yet to coalesce around agreed upon authors, methods, and texts, this work is vital for present and future considerations. Most Christian theologians, assuming they have had proper theological formation, can see how their thought fits into one of the above schemes. Read in concert with Niebuhr's seminal work, the positions can be expanded, so that the thinker who aligns more with Tertullian might see how her theology would reject technology while the thinker more in line with Calvin sees the paradox of the two.

1. This essay originally appeared in a different form as Checketts, "The Sacrality of Things," 130–152.

As we will see in the second volume of this work, the typological formulation has its limitations. Ellul, for example, is a Reformed theologian and quite Augustinian in his views, yet he does not fit into the "Christ transformer of culture" paradigm. Rather, as Schuurman already notes above, Ellul tends to embrace a more purely antithetical stance. Others, we will see, recognize technology in a more ambivalent way, or approach technology in a casuistic rather than categorical valuation of it.

As far as methods go, Niebuhr's typologies are useful tools, but we must not get the idea that they encompass the entirety of theological positions, nor even that any given theologian will fall neatly into one category or another. Karl Rahner, to take but one example, argues in his "The Experiment with Man" that human use of biotechnology is legitimate, as long as it is ordered toward Building the Kingdom of God.[2] Thus, Rahner appears to take a "Christ above culture" position, assuming technology merely needs to be subsumed to the proper ends. A mere two years later, however, he argued in "The Problem of Genetic Manipulation" that procreation should never be separated from marital sexual intercourse, taking a stronger "Christ against culture" position.[3] This position is hardly inconsistent, though it does not fit Niebuhr's typology: official Catholic magisterial tends to recognize the same view as Rahner. Indeed, as Mark Graham notes, despite Catholic theological ethics being a rich and varied tradition, it's position on technology tends to be entirely based on a given technology's *use*.[4] As such, the natural law-based system, as Paul Durbin will note in the next volume, tends to disfavor biotechnologies, especially those related to the beginnings and ends of life. And though Catholic Social Teaching emerges within the context of the Industrial Revolution, nothing like Ellul's assessment of "technique" exists in mainstream Catholic theology.

We should also note that methods that were once accepted often lose their relevance as a discipline develops and advances. Anthropology, for example, has in recent years come to grips with the racist assumptions that founded the discipline. Instead of a—typically white upper-middle class—lone scholar studying a culture as he makes of it in *his own* context, the field now emphasizes that there is not a neutral position from which to study another culture and that cultures themselves are

2. Rahner, *Theological Investigations* IX, 205–224

3. Rahner, *Theological Investigations* IX, 225–252.

4. Graham, "Technology and the Catholic Ethic of Use," 3.

not monolithic entities. Likewise, in a vein closer to the present study, philosophy of technology went from questions about the character of technology and humanity's relation to it to empirical analyses of the particular ways technologies do mediate our existence in what some call the "Empirical Turn."

In the present essay, I take up something like an "empirical turn" for theological studies of technology. Informed, as the philosophers of technology were, by methodological and case studies in Science and Technology Studies (STS), I assume that particular technologies and religious beliefs and practices need to be examined in their particularity before broad assumptions can be imposed upon them. Indeed, as I argue elsewhere, an STS model of the world, such as that of Actor-Network Theory, is critical for theological studies more generally, and especially for well-informed theological ethics of technology.[5] In line with this, I argue, through this paper, that an important new direction for theological studies of technology is to see technologies and Christian faith as co-constructing each other rather than existing as their own distinct spheres.

The Problem of "Christianity" and "Technology"

The reason for this shift is easily illustrated through the ambiguity of language itself. If we ask the question, "What should the Christian attitude toward technology be?" we note several assumptions underlying it. First, the question itself is normative, perhaps ethical (though that is not apparent by the grammar or vocabulary of the question), and assumes one or a few correct answers. This aspect itself is not nearly so troublesome, since the preceding essays all make the case on their own for why one answer rather than another should be accepted. However, there is ambiguity related to the two key terms of the sentence: Christian and technology. What do we mean, exactly, by these words?

Technology seems to be the more frustrating of the two. A reader at present (2022) would be unlikely to doubt that machine learning and computer programs for image recognition are "technology," but a typewriter, such as the original authors of this book likely all used, is more likely to appear to us as an archaeological artifact. Indeed, "artifacts" in the strictest sense of the word, are one major aspect of technology, such as the new iPhone or a Tesla electric roadster, but we also speak of less

5. Checketts, "The Cross and the Computer," 116–127.

concrete elements, such as "artificial intelligence" or the Internet. Often, as we see above in Schuurman's essay, technology means all tools human beings use. It is also not uncommon to see technology used to mean post-Industrial technology, as Ellul articulates it *The Technological Society*. Because of this difficulty, Pinch, Ashmore and Mulkay offer the "indexical" meaning of technology as well—in a Wittgensteinian vein, technology does not have a clear-cut definition but rather functions to mean various things depending on the context, all of which are related.[6]

I do not take such an ambiguous position. I define technology as something (whether a physical tool, a social system or even new organisms) created by human beings to channel power, typically to accomplish some end (though the success of attaining a particular end varies). This definition accommodates obvious meanings of technology as well as less obvious ones including artifacts, like a saw, an airplane, or a radio; social practices like discipline or propaganda; or even larger technological systems such as a factory, which combines discipline and machinery with economics. The accuracy or completeness of this definition can be debated, but it suffices to discuss most cases of what we ordinarily mean by technology. The reader will notice that this definition rejects the "social force" definition that one finds in the thought of Ellul or Heidegger. This is necessary for the foregoing discussion: as Bruno Latour argues, social *explanations* are merely means of avoiding the difficult task of *describing* how things happen.[7] If I aim to demonstrate that Christianity and technology exist dialogical relation, it falls on me to describe situations in which this happens.

The term "Christian" seems facetiously easier to define. However, "Christian" functions both as a demonym and as an adjective, so to say "Christian attitude" can either mean the attitude of Christians or the attitude that is proper to Christianity. The former makes sense when we consider the function of "should" in the question—we assume that there is already an attitude proper to Christianity which Christians themselves should adopt. However, this assume an answer to the latter, which is, in fact, the very heart of the debate. What is "Christianity" though, in this context? It might mean any of the following. First, it can mean "the mystical body of Christ" or the community of believers throughout the world. Second, it means the social institution of the Church, an institution which

6. Pinch, Ashmore, and Mulkay, "Technology, Testing, Text," 265.

7. Latour, *Reassembling the Social*, 150.

ordains leaders, regulates membership and teaching, is subject to laws and is often physically located in church buildings. Third, Christianity means the social force of the Christian ethos, a force Kierkegaard often polemicizes with the label "Christendom" over and against the community of full-faith "Christians." Fourth, Christianity means Christian theology, or the tradition of faith which Christian believers are to hold and churches are to preach. The final sense seems to be most appropriate, given that the subject here is "theology and technology."

In this essay, I demonstrate how Christianity, as the deposit of faith, is augmented by technology, especially technological development. I do not claim this is necessarily *good*; in the concluding section I illustrate how theology has occasionally positioned itself to *oppose* technologies rather than conform to them. Nonetheless, theology clearly develops alongside technology and the sphere of religious belief and the deposit of faith are *augmented* by technological advancement. Based on this conclusion, I advance a stronger, though more tentative claim: many technologies cross the boundary between what might be considered sacred and profane and become either sacramental or produce sacred artifacts. This claim requires a more careful articulation of the distinction between sacred and profane, which I provide in the penultimate section. As such, the salient point here is that rather than Christianity and technology existing as two spheres which we must consider as irreconcilable or complementary or compatible, we ought to see that they do not exist independently of each other at all: Christian theology is only understandable through a variety of technological means, just as much of modern technology is inextricably tied to its religious moorings.

I proceed in this claim by first examining the cases of three important technologies and their relationship with Christianity: the cross and Christology, the printing press and biblical studies, and transoceanic navigation and missiology. The fact that these technologies augment the realm of sacred theology, however, opens us to a new question, one which Mitcham raises in his introductory essay, namely the place of the sacred and profane in technology. I take a different tack from him, noting that, while it is true that the sacred subsumes what is profane so that technological artifacts can also be sacred artifacts, the specific manner in which a technology sacralizes or profanes is one of negotiation. I conclude this essay by suggesting that sacred technological artifacts, while possible, can only arise in specific circumstances, and thus cannot be expected, while *sacramental* technologies will undoubtedly multiply as long as Christians faithfully seek understanding in dialogue with new technologies.

Ave Crux Spes Unica—the Cross

In the novel *Men Like Gods*, H. G. Wells writes about a group of travelers who are transported to a parallel universe where human beings have used science and technology to escape human drudgery. When the travelers are granted an audience with Uthred, the leader of the utopians, Father Amerton asks whether they had a Jesus figure. The earthlings are told that there was such a person who was eventually killed on a turning wheel.[8] Wells's point is to lampoon Christian theology as overly superstitious—Uthred assures the travelers that he follows the teaching of this prophet but does not worship him—but an interesting point is made at the same time: the execution wheel becomes the symbol of the Christ figure of this alternate universe mimicking the Christian veneration of the Roman crucifix.

Crucifixion was a common practice utilized by the Roman Empire, as well as other ancient empires including the Persians, Greeks, and Jews. Roman crucifixion was carried out on criminals and revolutionaries who were typically of lower-class status.[9] The practice was primarily used in colonized regions of the empire and not Rome itself. Crucifixion was therefore a technology of discipline intended to keep unruly peoples in line.[10] Crucifixion functions as a technology according to the definition I laid out above: it functions as an artificial system to direct social behavior (or political power) in a totalizing fashion.[11] The crucified would suffer for hours or days as they waited to asphyxiate and were often crucified in highly visible locations. Typically, they were given no burial and were

8. Wells, *Men Like Gods*, Chapter the Fifth, Section 5.

9. Hengel, *Crucifixion*, 34 and 39.

10. See: Hughes, "Dishonour, Degradation and Display: Crucifixion in the Roman World," 3–4; Josephus, *The Wars of the Jews*, V, 11, 1–2.

11. One may note Michel Foucault refers to penal and disciplinary techniques as technologies by which the powerful control the unruly lower classes. Thus, while a particular form of execution may not, at first glance, seem like a technology, it is utilized in the same way that other technologies are. In this case, technology most closely means a type of knowledge, or a system of persons and apparatus designed to channel power a certain way. See Foucault, *Discipline and Punish*.

left to decompose where they were hung.[12] A lack of burial, combined with the suffering of the condemned and the high visibility of the punishment contributed to make this the most excruciating and shameful means of execution available to the Romans. The threat of this agonizing and shameful death, so the Romans supposed, would *deter* potential criminals, an argument that today is still employed to justify the use of capital punishment in the United States. Thus, crucifixion functions as an important technology of colonizing unruly peoples.

Nonetheless, the crucifix, in all its grisly and oppressive technological force is also perhaps the most obvious sacred technology. Most of the historical knowledge available on the technology of crucifixion is articulated or carried out in the context of better understanding the story of Jesus of Nazareth. The death of Jesus on the cross is a central part of the Gospel narrative, and an important element of the faith of Christians. The graphic scene of Christ crucified, hung on church walls or worn around worshipers' necks, is the subject of adoration, inspiration, veneration and exaltation. Many churches claim to possess a relic of the True Cross, and Christians across Christendom kneel before the cross on Good Friday. Indeed as in Wells's fictional account, this instrument of political power is *the* symbol of Christianity.

What's more, the cross itself plays a crucial role in Christology and soteriology. As Jean-Pierre Dupuy notes, Jesus's death at the hands of the Romans, intended to pacify the Jewish mob, results in Christianity, giving Christians a savior who is victorious while victim.[13] While the details of Christology and soteriology admit of differences of opinion, all prominently feature the cross, and most sacralize it. The central message of *Christus Victor* is contextualized through the ignominy of suffering the most shameful of deaths reserved for the most wretched. Since at least Anselm of Canterbury's articulation of the doctrine of substitutionary atonement, most Western Christians have believed that because of and through Christ's death their sins are remitted; Christ takes on their sins and acts as a perfect sacrifice to appease God.[14] John Calvin speaks of Christ's roles as prophet, priest and king—the priest function being upheld in Jesus offering himself as a sacrifice on the cross.[15] Even

12. Hengel, *Crucifixion*, 87

13. Dupuy, *The Mark of the Sacred*, 118.

14. Anselm of Canterbury, *Cur Deus Homo*, II, 14.

15. Calvin, *Institutes of the Christian Religion*, II, 15, 6.

Walter Rauschenbusch, whose "Social Gospel" eschews substitutionary atonement, reckons with the soteriological meaning of Christ's wrongful execution as a result of numerous social sins.[16]

A Christianity without the cross might look more like Buddhism—the leader preaches his dharma for decades before dying an unfortunate, though natural, death. Indeed, an important element of Christian orthodoxy, which separates Christians from Muslims or some Gnostics, is belief in Jesus's undeserved and premature death at the hands of the Roman Empire. Christianity in all of its creedal forms involves a profound recognition of the mystery of Christ's death, a death carried out through technological means, though the significance and importance vary by confession. I should note that modern Christian ethicists by and large condemn modern execution technologies as antichristian, but there would be *no* Christianity so-called (that is, no Christology) and no clear belief in the remittance of sins (soteriology) without this sacred technology. The doctrines held in the areas of Christology and soteriology maintain that Christ's death is a central component in both who he is as Christ and how he is able to remit our sins. Moreover, these two branches of theology are arguably (along with the doctrine of the trinity) the most unique elements of Christianity. Thus, it may not be too much to claim that Christianity gains its status as a unique revelation and a unique system of belief *through* this gruesome technology, that is, the technology is a *sine qua non* for Christianity *as* Christianity and not merely a branch of Judaism.

In the Beginning Was the Word—Printing

The second technology I wish to present is also quite apparent. Language itself has a fairly obvious, though no less wondrous, sacred function. None of the major world religions would have survived without both spoken and written language. The Qur'an, the Bhagavad Gita, the Torah, the Book of Mormon and the Pali Cannon are all key texts in important world religions, and in some cases the text functions as the primary medium of veneration, such as the Torah for Jews and the Qur'an for Muslims. No less is true with Christians and the Bible. Indeed, John the Evangelist writes "In the beginning was the Word, and the Word was with God, and the Word was God" (John 1:1).

16. Rauschenbusch, *A Theology for the Social Gospel*, 247.

Language is sacred, and it comes as no surprise that monasteries functioned as important repositories of literature—that is language—in the Middle Ages. Monks wrote, copied and preserved the deposit of literature and thought from which the Western Christian ethos is shaped.[17] Developments such as the Carolingian miniscule and the illuminated manuscript facilitated that writing process, but literacy and access to the scripture remained largely the privilege of the clergy—and not all of them at that—for hundreds of years. The problem of limited access to the sacred text became worse as vernacular languages developed but the Catholic Church—that is, Western Christianity by and large—still maintained the Vulgate Bible and Latin mass, which Roman Catholics still maintained until reforms instituted by the Second Vatican Council in 1965. Thus, by the fifteenth century, both liturgy and the Bible were inaccessible largely to all but the most well-educated. When the unlearned attended mass, they were unable to understand either the words of the ritual itself or the proclaimed word of God. Indeed, a popular belief, started perhaps by Anglican Bishop John Tillotson in 1687, suggests that the magic incantation "hocus pocus" was a corruption of the Latin words spoken at the moment of sacrifice in the Mass, "*Hoc est corpus meum*."[18] The ritual symbolism and meaning became obscured through linguistic misunderstanding, and the (Latin) language went beyond its technical function to take on supernatural or sacred significance, which, one might note, Latin seems to hold to this day.[19]

The 1439 invention of the printing press changed much of this. Although the Church was originally hesitant to embrace printing, it quickly became the primary client of printers across Europe. Printing was efficient for accurately and quickly producing Missals, Lectionaries, Confessionals, and numerous scholarly works to be read in church-sponsored universities. More significantly, the widespread use of printing presses 500 years ago, as opposed to their non-existence 600 years ago, is one of the primary factors for why Martin Luther's reformation in 1517

17. In some cases, monks and monasteries were important for introducing or *re*-introducing texts into the Western canon. Consider, for example, the work of Saints Albert the Great and Thomas Aquinas in reintroducing Latin translations of Aristotle, received from Muslim scholars after the West had lost Aristotle's thought, into the academy.

18. Tillotson, *An Answer to Discourse against Transubstantiation*, 74.

19. Not only can one see this in many of the trappings of academic writing ("i.e.," "pace," "sic," "etc."), but one even sees this in popular culture, where Latin is often used in magical formulas, demonic conjuring or holy rituals.

was successful and Jan Huss's of 1412 was not.[20] Luther's provocative 95 Theses, meant to start a dialogue in Wittenberg, were quickly spread throughout the region due to the ease of mass production through printing. While Luther attracted the ire of the Catholic magisterium, he also attracted the interest and patronage of numerous German aristocrats who saved his life from papist forces and allowed him to continue his work as a reformer.

While protected from antagonistic papal forces, Luther translated the Bible from copies of the original Greek and Hebrew texts into German in an effort to make the text more accessible to the laity. This move would be important for Luther's teaching of *sola scriptura*—a belief that Scripture alone had the truth. Against the Catholic method of a primarily oral transmission of both scripture and its meaning, Luther's followers believed in the need for an uninterpreted text. The publication of the Bible in German was a tremendous success at the time, selling thousands of copies across Germania, and also, in effect, setting a standard for the German language.[21] Luther also used the printing press to print pamphlets, including his own theological writings and his sermons and homilies, many of which were in German.[22] The style of Protestant theology and its survival in formerly Catholic countries owe much of their success to the ease of access granted by Gutenberg's printing press in Germania and beyond.

The printing press effected at least two major theological shifts. First, it was catalyst for the systematization and development of biblical studies. The Catholic Church, up until Vatican II, maintained the Latin Vulgate as the official Bible of the faith.[23] Luther, however, encouraged people to read the text in their own native language. Additionally, Catholicism has long maintained the importance of Tradition and scripture in theology, with a *de facto* preference for Tradition. The Protestant Reformation encouraged theologians and pastors to return to the text and esteem it above the Tradition that interpreted it. In the Protestant principle of *sola scriptura*, the literal text of the Bible became more important than its interpretation, no matter how well-esteemed the interpreter was, and

20. Holborn, "Printing and the Growth of a Protestant Movement in Germany from 1517 to 1524," 123–137.

21. See Schreiber, "Deutsche for Sale," 195.

22. Crofts, "Printing, Reform, and the Catholic Reformation in Germany (1521-1545)," 369–381.

23. Paul VI, *Dei Verbum*, 22.

historical-critical readings of the text and close readings of the original Greek and Hebrew manuscripts soon followed. The ease of access facilitated by the printing press made possible the personal and professional study of both vernacular and classical-language texts. Studying the Bible no longer required one to live close to a monastery and read Latin.

Second, Luther's propagation of his Bible and his own sermons paved the way for new liturgical styles. To this day, Protestantism is perhaps most easily contrasted against Catholicism liturgically by its emphasis on the word preached from the pulpit over the Eucharist consecrated on the altar; the spoken and written, and thus reproducible, word has taken priority over the communal sharing of the body and blood of Christ.[24] Luther's own distribution of vernacular sermons made homiletics available to the laity and shifted the role of the pastor from being primarily a ritual performer (i.e. priest) to being a homilist (evangelizer). Thus, the technology of printing became an important tool for bringing the word of God to the laity, both in the printed Bible and in spoken sermons, although from a Catholic perspective this serves an ambiguous function; in a modern context this accessibility is to be commended, but the fracturing of the Western Church which the Protestant Reformation represents is inextricable from this fact.

Go and Make Disciples of All Nations—Transoceanic Navigation

The final technology I wish to lift up is far less obvious than the first two. In the early fifteenth century, after the collapse of the Mongol Empire and the Abbasid Caliphate, Spanish and Portuguese traders looked for new ways to open up trade with India. Borrowing such technologies as advanced cartography, improved ship design and trigonometry from North African Muslims, and adopting the use of the ancient astrolabe and the newer sextant and magnetic compass, sailors were able to venture farther

24. Catholics celebrate mass on all days of the year except Good Friday, though Good Friday worship includes partaking of Eucharist consecrated on Maundy Thursday as part of Easter Triduum. Many Protestant worship services (e.g. Presbyterian, Baptist, Evangelical, Methodist) celebrate communion on a *monthly* basis. More notably, Catholic homilies tend to be around ten minutes in length, while it would be uncommon for an average adult Protestant sermon to be less than twenty-five or thirty minutes long. Of course, there are congregations where this is different, such as Anglicans or charismatic Catholic congregations.

away from Europe than ever before, eventually stumbling across other inhabited continents. The combination of these various technologies constituted a larger technological system, one which has been improved but has remained in use for the past five hundred years, namely transoceanic navigation.

The first conquistadors were nominally Catholic, operating under the blessing of the pope and often accompanied by chaplains. Of course, their work was carried out for the benefit of the Portuguese and Spanish crowns and has deep implications for the shaping of world markets, cultural paradigms, and the industrial system, but conquistadors also enjoyed religious support. In 1514, one chaplain, Bartolome de las Casas, had a profound conversion experience while ministering in South America, and, after receiving a new commission from Pope Paul III, began proselytizing to the Native South Americans. Other clergy followed suit, and the term "mission," as a foreign base of ministry, was coined nine years later when twelve friars were sent to the New World as "missionaries."[25] Following this, specially dedicated Catholic and Protestant missionaries have traveled to Asia, Africa and Oceania as well to spread Christianity. For the last 500 years, missionary work and missiology has typically meant itinerant ministry as a calling and has often evoked images of work in foreign lands. Thus, while distant evangelism has always been a feature of Christianity, the vocation of transcontinental ministry and the subsequent system of evangelical operations in foreign lands truly gets its genesis only as recently as the sixteenth century.

Many early Jesuit missionaries were educated in advanced mathematics and navigation as part of their educational regimen before their ordinations. In turn, due to their calling to "set the world on fire," they were quite often willing to share their scientific and technological knowledge with the peoples they encountered. Jesuit missionaries to China first presented advanced mathematics and astronomical tools to Chinese dignitaries, later completed cartographical surveys as a ministry in their missionary work, and sometimes held maps as relic-like keepsakes.[26] The work of God, in the Jesuitical worldview was furthered by the technological implements connected to navigation. Thus, not only did the transoceanic navigational technology provide the condition for missionary work

25. Clossey, *Salvation and Globalization in the Early Jesuit Missions*, 13.

26. Clossey, *Salvation and Globalization in the Early Jesuit Missions*, 13.

to begin, but it also instantiated itself in various ways as reliquary and evangelical treasures for those proselyting foreign land.

The Jesuits' missionary work was further animated by an apocalyptic zeal that arrived with the Age of Discovery. Many missionaries and theologians considered the "discovery" of the New World to be an oracle of sorts to the end times. They believed that Christ's Second Coming would not arrive until *all* the world, including those non-Christians Europeans had recently encountered (i.e. Native Americans, Southeast Asians and Pacific Islanders, and southern Africans), had heard the Gospel message. The encounter with new races of human beings, ignorant entirely of Jesus Christ, provided not only a new arena, but also a new impetus to evangelical work.[27] The fullness of God's reign, for which Christians have long waited in joyful hope, could only be triggered by missionary work to the far reaches of the world. Thus, the technologies integrated in the exploratory endeavors of early-modern Europeans became the harbingers of new understandings both of the calling to preach the Gospel (previously carried out primarily in European Christendom and among European peoples) and the advent of the Eschaton.

This fervor did not only persist with the Jesuit missionaries; it also regained energy through new Reformation movements, including Methodism, Evangelicalism and Mormonism, each of which has emphasized transcontinental evangelism as a foundational part of their ecclesiology. To this day, many Christian churches send missionaries, either as evangelizers or as humanitarians, to foreign lands to carry out their call from God. The technological system of transoceanic travel, including the development of reliable maps, accurate means of measuring both latitude and longitude, and advanced sailboat construction were necessary for accomplishing this missionary work, but are often forgotten or remain *invisible* in the narrative of Christian history. For example, by the time Presbyterian and Methodist missionaries traveled to Korea in the 1880s, transcontinental travel had disappeared into the background in which foreign ministry is situated.[28] Missionaries like Horace Grant Underwood, who

27. Clossey, *Salvation and Globalization in the Early Jesuit Missions*, 95.

28. It would be remiss of me if I neglected to mention that Korea was the first nation to have its own denizens bring Christianity from abroad. Korea is a highly Confucian nation, and Confucian scholars from the Joseon dynasty (ca. 1500–1890) often studied in Beijing, where some encountered the writings of Matteo Ricci and Christian writings. Korea experienced a truly grassroots spread of Christianity in the early 1800s, resulting in the mass persecutions from 1840–1850 because of Christians' refusal to practice ancestor worship, a major component of Joseon Confucian public

founded Yonsei University, and Mary F. Scranton, who founded Ewha Women's University, lived in a world already replete with missionaries, both Protestant and Catholic, transnavigating oceans for evangelical aims—their own participation fit within pre-established norms, which allowed them to establish hospitals and educational institutions with ease. Nonetheless, the entire theological field of missiology as a theological discipline, complete with considerations to *whom* to preach and *how* to preach, is dependent upon the highly technical navigational systems developed over the course of the fifteenth century. Moreover, certain understandings of eschatology, including the task of the believers before the arrival of end times, and the meaning of "all the world" which should be brought to Christ (Cf Mark 16:15) are re-contextualized with the advent of global transversal technologies.

Few people would argue thus far that these three technologies have not had profound impacts on shaping Christianity to be what it is today. The cross and the printing press have each garnered a great deal of attention from historians and theologians, as noted in the citations for each of those technologies. Transoceanic navigation, remains both the least obvious and the least sacred of the three examined. And yet, its influence on present-day Christianity is undeniable. There is, of course, no Christianity at all without Jesus of Nazareth executed on a cross, and, as the example of Jan Hus suggests, there might be no Protestantism without, at the very least, the printing press. As such, these two stand out as paradigmatic in their own regard. Navigation, however, often conjures images of conquest, colonialism and empire—not the typical realms of the sacred. Indeed, Jacques Ellul himself notes that navigation, "directed by the will to power and exploitation, *could not* have produced any result other than the one that has been lived (colonialism)."[29] Yet the story of Jesuit,

religion. This resulted in the beheading of Korea's patron saint, the first ordained Korean priest, Andrew Taegon Kim (died September 16, 1846). The Joseon kingdom martyred between 10,000 and 20,000 Christians, and eventually tolerated Christianity. Shortly after, Catholic prelates gave permission for Korean Catholics to practice ancestor worship, noting that it resembled veneration of saints. When Protestant missionaries arrived in Korea thirty years later, these obstacles were absent, allowing an ease in missionary work unprecedented before. A peculiar consequence of this is that Jeoldusan Martyr's Shrine, the site where Kim and over 1,000 others were beheaded in Seoul on the Han River, borders to the west of Yangwahin Foreign Missionary Cemetery, where are interred the above mentioned Underwood, as well as Henry Appenzeller, Homer Hubert and William James Hall, among others. See, e.g., Buswell and Lee, *Christianity in Korea*.

29. Ellul, "The Relationship between Man and Creation," volume II of this work,

Franciscan, Dominican, Methodist, Presbyterian, and other Christian missionaries in traveling to distant lands through the use of navigational technologies to carry out their sacred calling belies this conclusion. We thus turn to an interesting, yet difficult problem: if these technologies can be sacred in their own right, what is it that makes a technology sacred?

Sacred Technologies or Sacramental Technologies?

The above survey tells us that technologies do and can have a positive impact on Christian faith. But do they go beyond the typologies of Niebuhr? Let us ask a different question: what do these technologies tell us about the relationship between the realm of the technological and the realm of the sacred? Clearly, they each have notable impact on the development of certain branches of theology—modern Christian understandings of soteriology, the reading of the Bible, and the call to mission are contextualized by the function of the technologies of the cross, the printing press and transoceanic navigation. However, this does not tell us that they are sacred, nor even how we can measure sacrality. Emile Durkheim defines the sacred against the profane—what is sacred is set apart from what is profane.[30] This, Durkheim assures us, is not to mean that what is profane is bad or demonic as the realm of the demons in fact another sort of sacred.[31] Rather, the sacred and the profane are incompatible with each other; what is sacred cannot come into contact with the profane, nor can the profane survive contact with the sacred. If they should meet, either the sacred will be profanized or the profane will be obliterated by the sacred. The "sacred" then appears rather as we might think of magic, or better, as "enchantment" in the sense Charles Taylor suggests, namely that certain artifacts, places, persons or acts refute profane explanations and must be understood as set apart.[32]

Moreover, Durkheim talks about the categories of sacred and profane as describing objects within the world.[33] A chalice may be sacred, or an altar, but a system or procedure is not sacred, unless the system or procedure itself is designated sacred through its incorporation of sacred

emphasis original.

30. Durkheim, *Elementary Forms*, 32.

31. Durkheim, *Elementary Forms*, 175.

32. Taylor, *A Secular Age*, 26.

33. Durkheim, *Elementary Forms*, 34 and 110.

objects.[34] Thus, artifacts may be once and always sacred, but technological systems or knowledge is not inherently sacred. The ritual sacrifice may be a sacred act but killing a lamb in another context is profane. A pilgrimage may be sacred, but any other journey is not. A meal shared between friends is profane; a meal shared among the community of faith, led by a priest, carried out in a sacred place is Eucharist. Mitcham uses an example in his introductory essay which is illustrative: the monastery uses disciplinary techniques which can be profane but when ordered to the formation of monks are sacred. On the other hand, the ritual knife remains sacred in all contexts—it emits the holy. Thus, the sacred tends to fall primarily upon concrete objects, that is, particular vessels, garments, edifices, persons and animals, and only contextually upon systems or knowledge. The Priestly Code in Leviticus includes many practical suggestions for preparing slaughtered animals for consumption, but when these are followed by particular persons (priests) in a particular place (the tabernacle or the temple) in particular times (holy days like Yom Kippur or Passover), the act becomes a *sacrifice* (literally "making holy").

The question of separate spheres of Christianity and technology relies on this distinction between the sacred and the profane, with the *de facto* assumption that (modern) technologies are profane. An extension of this, the "Christ against culture" argument illustrated by Blair, Ellul and others, is that technologies themselves *profanize* by either interrupting the domain of the sacred or by competing for domination. Albert Borgmann seems most direct about this; in both *Technology and the Character of Contemporary Life* and *Power Failure: Christianity in the Culture of Technology*, he notes that technologies commodify what would ordinarily be sacred. Moreover, he adds that through a rededication to sacralizing certain moments and experiences ("focal points") which have otherwise become profane, Christians can regain a sense of the sacred.[35] Thus, for Borgmann, the character of technology resists the sacred and the nature of sacrality requires resistance against technology. Mitcham adds to this that technologies which otherwise might replace older ones in mundane settings, such as e-book readers instead of books, electric lightbulbs instead of candles, and projector slides instead of pamphlets, are out of place in sacred rituals, and, in some cases, plainly absurd. After reading the Gospel in Mass, for example, the priest or lector kisses the

34. Durkheim, *Elmentary Forms*, 194.

35. See his essay in the second volume of this work.

lectionary, an act that becomes sacrilegious if the text is on an electronic tablet.[36] It seems that some technologies (artifacts or systems) certainly resist sacralization, or, at the very least, cannot be said to be sacred in an unequivocal sense, while other technologies should. A consecrated rosary or crucifix is sacred in any setting; the same cannot be said about an iPhone.[37]

Two important distinctions must therefore be made about the preceding observations on the intersection of theology and technology. First, one must be willing to grant that some technologies are sacred, while others can be said to be merely "sacramental." Sacramentals are "sacred signs which bear a resemblance to the sacraments: they signify effects, particularly of a spiritual kind, which are obtained through the Church's intercession."[38] A technology cannot be a "sacramental" in a strict sense unless declared such by the Church, but, in a more liberal sense, all of the technologies examined in the above sections are at least "sacramental" insofar as they are means by which men and women can experience God's grace. The printing press made the Bible accessible to men and women who otherwise lacked access to it; transoceanic navigation brought God's grace to entire new continents. The cross, however, remains a sacred technology insofar as the cross itself is a sacred object. Relics of the True Cross and crucifixes blessed by priests are sacred objects, even while evoking the originary disciplinary technological function of shameful execution, albeit subverted through the risen Christ. On the other hand, printing presses and compasses are not sacred. However, we should recognize that some people might view an original Gutenberg or Luther Bible as possessing the status of being a sacred artifact, and, as noted above, many Jesuit missionaries treated maps and navigational instruments as relics.

This leads to the second distinction: recall that technologies exist both as artifacts and as knowledge or procedures. The true cross, original

36. I have also discussed this scenario with numerous ordained priests in the Catholic Church. While many would find no problem reading the daily breviary through an electronic tablet, none feel that reading a digital lectionary would be appropriate at this time. See also Carl Mitcham, "Religion and Technology," 470; Carl Mitcham, "The Love of Technology is the Root of All Evils," 17–28.

37. Andres Serrano's 1987 art piece *Piss Christ* is provocative because of the way the artist deliberately profanes the sacred. A crucifix is meant to be adored or venerated; it is an icon. Submerging the icon in urine is an act of deliberately transgressing the boundaries of sacred and profane.

38. Paul VI, *Sacrosanctum Concilium*, 60.

Gutenberg Bibles and sixteenth century maps all have the status of being artifacts. They exist as concrete objects in the world. Crucifixion, printing and navigation, however, are all systems of knowledge. These exist as procedures or methods whereby one may accomplish a given task. The two cannot be fully separated from each other; there is no printing or navigation without printing presses or compasses, and the sign of the cross always refers to death by crucifixion. Nonetheless, crosses exist in a world mostly devoid of crucifixion, and the knowledge of printing has survived most of the original works printed. More importantly, however, people often use technological artifacts without having knowledge of their operation, while others may have technological knowledge without possession of the artifacts needed for that knowledge. An example of the former can be seen in the divide between people who know how to build or program a computer and all the people who own computers. An example of the latter may be men who were once boy scouts but now typically use matches or lighters rather than flint and steel to start fires.

At this point, it should become clear why I prefer to speak of technolog*ies* in particular instantiations rather than technolog*y* as a social force. The view of the essays above tends to follow the "classical philosophy of technology" preference for thinking of technology in monolithic terms.[39] But most of these thinkers rely on particular technologies to illustrate their view, including nuclear weapons (Mitcham and Schuurman), automobiles and airplanes (Malet), radios and televisions (Fudpucker and Malet) or computers (Schuurman). Indeed, it is notable that the two essayists who do not reference specific technologies are Tekippe and Blair; Tekippe primarily applies Lonergan's view of *science* to the broader question of technology, while Blair treats *technique* as a threat to Christianity. Inevitably, if one wishes to demonstrate their beliefs about the nature of technology, they must use examples of technology. If we attend to the study of specific technologies, then, instead of assuming all technology has a singular character, we find that the statement of the relationship between technology and Christianity is simultaneously overgeneralized while being understated. In contrast to the above thinkers, I suggest that there is neither a singular character of technology nor of Christianity: the dual-sphere model of profane technology and sacred Christianity is a false model.

39. Verbeek, *What Things Do*, 7.

To illustrate this point, I suggest using the distinctions laid out above to consider how technologies interact with the realm of the sacred. One can think about this open question under at least four categories: sacred artifacts, sacramental artifacts, sacred techniques (i.e., technical knowledge), and sacramental techniques. A sacred technique would be a technique relegated exclusively to the realm of the sacred. The priest's knowledge of the Eucharistic rite is non-transferable to a situation of public speaking; the icon writer's skill cannot be interchanged for the manufacturer's. In this sense, new sacred techniques would only arise if and when a technique is developed exclusively for use in sacred contexts, such as the evangelization methods of missionaries or the Catholic Worker's hospitality efforts. Sacramental artifacts would be any object which facilitates God's grace, and could range from printed devotional texts, plastic statues or even media technologies in certain contexts. An artifact would be sacred only as a particular, unique artifact, an object that has, as it were, an "aura" surrounding it. A Gutenberg Bible, a saint's relic, a consecrated chalice or a blessed medal may all have the status of being sacred objects, while replications or imitations of them do not. Finally, a sacramental technique would be knowledge that somehow facilitates God's grace, which may easily include artistic, transportive, communicative, medical, therapeutic or other systems of knowledge.

The technologies listed above are "sacralized" in two senses. First, they create sacred artifacts, including the most obvious true cross and devotional crucifixes, and the less obvious maps, navigational tools, and first edition prints of religious texts. Second, they are sacramental techniques: the knowledge of crucifixion techniques provides a means by which salvation is granted; printing facilitates a revolution in worship and biblical devotion; navigation allows the Gospel to be spread to all the world. It is important to note, then that new technologies not only have the ability to add to the list of sacred artifacts that clutter museums and churches; they also have the potential to augment the realm of God's grace. In this sense, knowledge of certain practices can and does change what falls under the purview of theological investigation. New technologies often create new theologies. Thus, the character of technologies, be they directed to capitalistic, militaristic or other profane goals, does not foreclose the possibility of them expanding the sacred by opening new opportunities for God's grace to be expanded. The "Christ against culture" model ultimately forgets that the Christian is called to be a Christian in an historical setting and to live out that Christian call in the particular constellation of persons, political and economic systems, knowledge bases and technologies which make up her life. Not only is technology not inherently against Christianity, it is always part of the constellation of the world the Christian must operate within, and particular technologies open new opportunities for encountering the Divine.

Conclusion: Modern Sacred Technologies?

At this point, I believe it is clear that the claim that Christians ought to completely oppose technology is misguided. It is quite clear that Christian theology, especially as a realm of inquiry into human relationship with the divine, has been augmented by, at the very least, the technologies listed above. Nonetheless, given that the most recent technology I highlight achieves its zenith in Magellan's circumnavigational voyage of 1519–1522, one might have the impression that modern technologies have nothing to add to the conversation. Indeed, the general focus of the above essays is on *modern* technologies, especially those following James Watt's improved steam engine of 1750. In this concluding section then, I wish first to suggest that modern technologies *can* sacralize, at least in the sense of sacramental techniques and, second, consider the prospect of technological artifacts being made sacred.

New technological artifacts will likely only become sacred through their contact with a saint or holy event. Blessed Carlo Acutis's Playstation 2 or home computer might be considered a secondary relic, for example. The possibility of a technological artifact becoming sacred presupposes sacred *people* expanding the circle of the sacred through their use of particular technological objects, but the point of this inquiry is to ascertain whether technologies themselves can alter the circle of the sacred. Thus, most sacred artifacts will expand the sacred not through their own merit, but rather through the merits of those who interact with the technology. Such would seem to be the case anyway in light of the cross, first edition Gutenberg Bibles, or the maps Jesuit missionaries held in reverence. The real question therefore is whether we will see sacramental techniques, and not only sacred artifacts.

As a way to begin addressing this question, one may look at the considerations of theologians reflecting on the significance of the Internet. Certainly, the Internet as a technology has more *profane* about it than it does sacred—from pornography to consumeristic shopping, from competitive gaming to cyberbullying on social media, the experience of most users of the Internet is not a deeply sacred one. Yet, some theologians contend that the Internet has a role in shaping or augmenting the realm of the sacred. Nathan D. Mitchell notes that, just as previous communications revolutions changed liturgy, so might the Internet, perhaps by changing the medium of the word.[40] Thomas Boomershine suggests the Internet has already changed the way the Word of God is received by worshipers away from a primarily personal, literary style characteristic of the Enlightenment—wrought, in part, by the advent of the same printing press—to a "post-literary," active and performative style characteristic of multi-media presentations.[41] Antonio Spadaro consider the ambiguity of Internet "communion"—what does it mean to communicate with others online and how does this relate to our Christian notions of interpersonal interaction?[42] Elizabeth Drescher notes that social media change our experience with the deceased other, by offering the dying the opportunity to more easily express their experience and by offering distant others the possibility to respond to the dying or deceased.[43] Each of these theologians notes that the Internet changes our own experience of what is sacred and requires an appropriate adjustment of the realm of the sacred in kind. Although in some cases, the possibility of redemption is bleak Spadaro aptly notes that the communal experience of Sacrament that Catholics share at the Mass is ultimately impossible in a virtual setting—these theologians all see the realm of the sacred not being destroyed or threatened, but adapting to new technologies.[44]

Technologies do, therefore, *change* the realm of the sacred. As a collective, they are not inherently opposed to the sacred, though some may compete for our attention or resist sacralization. It is hard to find God in a nuclear silo or sweatshop, though areas of theology like the Social Gospel movement and the just war indicate the noncircumscribable nature of God. Ultimately, the sacred remains a big enough category that

40. Mitchell, "Ritual and New Media," 95.

41. Boomershine, "The Embodiment of the Word," 15–19.

42. Spadaro, *Friending God*, Chapter 7: Who Is Our Neighbor Online?

43. Drescher, "Pixels Perpetual Shine," 204–218.

44. Two further examples are illustrative as well. With the COVID 19 pandemic beginning in 2020, many Christians across the world had to experience liturgy primarily online for months. Second, Carlo Acutis, beatified October 10, 2020, has, as his cause for canonization, the use of the Internet for evangelizing primarily by creating web pages dedicated to the Sacraments.

experience of the Divine is possible with new technologies. New forms of technology and new techniques open new possibilities for experiencing the divine. Indeed, this is the task of theology, especially when theology reflects upon new technologies. On this front, the work of the authors in this volume and the next is prescient: they recognize the great need for theological reflection upon the world ever changed by new technologies. Thus, the greater question that remains is whether new profane technologies can be sacralized or "baptized" into Christianity—that is, whether a technology can itself be put to serve primarily the purposes of Christianity rather than profane purposes. The question is not whether one can experience the sacred alongside or utilizing new technologies, but whether these technologies can be intentionally directed toward sacred ends.

I submit the possibility for a "baptized" technology is yet open. Pierre Teilhard de Chardin, for example, saw wonder in both the atomic bomb and E. O. Lawrence's cyclotrons, modern technologies the consequences of which cost hundreds of thousands of people their lives and brought the world to chaos for the better part of a century.[45] One may disagree with Teilhard's often eccentric mystical perspective, but other theologians have also seen the possibility of new technologies carrying out Christian social and moral duties, such as alleviating poverty and suffering or curing illness.[46] Whether golden rice will be seen as a sacred technology is an open question, but a great strength of Christianity lies in its ability to incorporate what is often seen as endemic to its mission. One only need look back to St Thomas Aquinas's appropriation of Aristotelian thought in the thirteenth century, or Augustine's adoption of Platonism in the fourth, to remember that Christianity has often sacralized what was previously profane.

I conclude simply that technology as a monolithic concept is not against Christianity. Some technologies, such as nuclear weapons, the factory system, or the strip mine, may manifest antichristian tendencies or open unchristian possibilities, but technology should not be so generalized to assume all instantiations are antitheistic. Moreover, Christianity itself shapes technologies that emerge: without the Catholic Church, the printing press would have developed more slowly; without church

45. Teilhard, "On Looking at a Cyclotron," 347–358; Teilhard, "Some Reflections on the Spiritual Repercussions of the Atom Bomb," 133–142.

46. See: Clarke, "Technology and Man," 250; Durbin's essay in Volume II of this work; Hefner, *Technology and Human Becoming*, 84–87; Barbour, *Ethics in an Age of Technology*, 81.

blessing, Spanish and Portuguese voyages would have been less emboldened; the architectural, communication and mechanical advancements in Europe in the Middle Ages all had religious backings. One must also not forget Christianity itself is a historically-oriented faith and thus owes its existence to particular constellations of technologies, human agents and other socially-relevant factors. Jesus of Nazareth lived in first century Palestine, where he taught and ministered to colonized Jews and died on a Roman crucifix. Technologies likewise are developed in historically-contingent circumstances: there is no universal "essence" of technology, only particular technologies emerging in particular settings. To claim some generalized "technology" is opposed to Christianity is thus to reduce both technology and Christianity and ignore their complicated, ambivalent history of mutual co-construction. Technology creates the sacred even if it simultaneously expands the realm of the profane.

The field of theology and technology, or theological studies of technology, which the initial printing of this book attempted to begin thirty-five years ago is still underdeveloped, unlike philosophy of technology. There is no "Society for Theology and Technology" yet, and the scholars thinking in this area are often diffuse and lack sufficient resources to advance the field. The essays in this book are indispensable for beginning this thinking, and they provide numerous frameworks and considerations that should not be dismissed. Nonetheless, it is my hope that we can go beyond a "classical" view and pursue an "empirical turn" like the field of philosophy of technology. I have attempted a beginning of this with the concrete examples discussed above, and it is my hope that other authors will further this theological inquiry. By examining the effects of particular technologies on "God-talk" (*theo-logos*), the field can avoid the temptation to withdraw from technology and better consider how technologies can expand the sacred, how to avoid the trappings of profanation, and how to bring theology into dialogue with technological development and social change.

Bibliography

Barbour, Ian. *Ethics in an Age of Technology*. San Francisco: HarperCollins, 1993.

Boomershine, Thomas. "The Embodiment of the Word: A Pastoral Approach to Scripture in a Digital Age." *Communications Research Trends* 37, no. 2 (2018) 15–19.

Borgmann, Albert. *Power Failure: Christianity in the Culture of Technology*. Grand Rapids: Brazos Press, 2003.

Buswell, Robert E., and Timothy S. Lee. *Christianity in Korea*. Honolulu: University of Hawai'i, 2006.

Calvin, John. *Institutes of the Christian Religion*. Translated by Henry Beveridge. Orlando: Signalman, 2009.

Checketts, Levi. "The Sacrality of Things: On the Technological Augmentation of the Sacred." *Techné: Research in Philosophy and Technology* 25, No. 1 (2021) 130–152.

———. "The Cross and the Computer: Actor-Network Theory and Christianity." *Theology and Science* 15, no. 1 (January 2017) 16–27.

Clarke, W. Norris. "Technology and Man: A Christian View." In *Philosophy and Technology Readings in the Philosophical Problems of Technology*, edited by Carl Mitcham and Robert Mackey, 247–258. New York: The Free Press, 1972.

Clossey, Luke. *Salvation and Globalization in the Early Jesuit Missions*. Cambridge: Cambridge University Press, 2008.

Crofts, Richard A. "Printing, Reform, and the Catholic Reformation in Germany (1521–1545)." *Sixteenth Century Journal* 16, no. 3 (1985) 369–381.

Drescher, Elizabeth. "Pixels Perpetual Shine: The Mediation of Illness, Dying and Death in the Digital Age." *CrossCurrents* 62, no. 2 (2012) 204–218.

Dupuy, Jean-Pierre. *The Mark of the Sacred*. Translated by M. B. Debevoise. Stanford: Stanford University Press, 2013.

Durkheim, Emile. *The Elementary Forms of the Religious Life*. Translated by Joseph Ward Swain. London: George Allen & Unwin, 1964.

Foucault, Michel. *Discipline and Punish: The Birth of the Prison*. Translated by Alan Sheridan. New York: Vintage Books, 1995.

Graham, Mark. "Technology and the Catholic Ethic of Use: Starting a New Conversation." *Journal of Religion, Theology and Technology* 3, no. 1 (November 2012) 1–21.

Hefner, Philip. *Technology and Human Becoming*. Minneapolis: Fortress Press, 2003.

Hengel, Martin. *Crucifixion*. Translated by John Bowden. Philadelphia: Fortress Press, 1977.

Holborn, Louise W. "Printing and the Growth of a Protestant Movement in Germany from 1517 to 1524." *Church History* 11, no. 2 (1942) 123–137.

Hughes, Philip John. "Dishonour, Degradation and Display: Crucifixion in the Roman World." *Harts and Minds: The Journal for Humanities and Arts* 1, no. 3 (2013) 1–24.

Latour, Bruno. *Reassembling the Social: An Introduction to Actor-Network-Theory*. Oxford: Oxford University Press, 2005.

Mitcham, Carl. "The Love of Technology is the Root of All Evils." *Epiphany* 8, no. 1 (1987) 17–28.

———. "Religion and Technology." In *A Companion to the Philosophy of Technology*, edited by Jan Kyrre Berg Olsen et al., 466–473. Malden, MA: Wiley-Blackwell, 2009.

Mitchell, Nathan D. "Ritual and New Media." *Concilium* 2005, no. 1 (2005) 90–98.

Paul VI. *Sacrosancturn Concilium*. Vatican City: Libreria Editrice Vaticana, 1963.

———. *Dei Verbum*. Vatican City: Libreria Editrice Vaticana, 1965.

Pinch, Trevor, Malcolm Ashmore, and Michael Mulkay. "Technology, Testing, Text: Clinical Budgeting in the U.K. National Health Service." In *Shaping Technology/Building Society: Studies in Sociotechnical Change*, edited by Wiebe E. Bijker and John Law, 265–289. Cambridge, MA: MIT Press, 1992.

Rauschenbusch, Walter. *A Theology for the Social Gospel.* New York: Cosimo Classics, 2012.

Rahner, Karl. *Theological Investigations IX: Writings of 1965–67.* Translated by Graham Harrison. New York: Herder & Herder, 1972.

Schreiber, Mathias. "Deutsche for Sale." *Der Spiegel* 40 (2006) 182–198.

Spadaro, Antonio, SJ. *Friending God: Social Media, Spirituality and Community.* Translated by Robert H. Hopcke. Chestnut Ridge, NY: Crossroad Publishing, 2016.

Taylor, Charles. *A Secular Age.* Cambridge, MA: Belknap Press, 2007.

Teilhard de Chardin, Pierre. On Looking at a Cyclotron." In *Activation of Energy,* translated by René Hague, 347–358. San Diego: Harcourt, 1978.

———. "Some Reflections on the Spiritual Repercussions of the Atom Bomb." In *The Future of Man,* translated by Norman Denny, 133–142. New York: Doubleday, 1964.

Tillotson, John. *An Answer to Discourse against Transubstantiation.* London: Henry Mills, 1687.

Verbeek, Peter-Paul. *What Things Do: Philosophical Reflections on Technology, Agency and Design.* Translated by Robert P. Crease. University Park, PA: Pennsylvania State University, 2000.

Wells, H. G. *Men Like Gods.* E-book edition. Adelaide: University of Adelaide, 2014.

Essay 8

Theology and Technology Revisited

Carl Mitcham

With Levi Checketts

On behalf of Jim Grote (1954–2013) and myself let me begin with thanks to Levi Checketts for reviving this volume and to Ted Lewis at Wipf & Stock for publication. We are honored, even if we no longer fully agree with all the original argument it presents. Given the intensified twenty-first-century presence of the religious in a lifeworld increasingly dominated by engineering and technology, we nevertheless trust that a new version of this forty-year-old project may contribute to further critical reflection on theology and technology.

Our collection of studies on technology as a theological-political problem was edited during the first term of American President Ronald Reagan. The editors were disaffected from the dominant Christian establishment but inspired by radical Christian ideals and found themselves surrounded by a conservative ascendency that was weaving a "moral majority" of fundamentalist resentment, neoliberal economics, and faith in technology into a newly aggressive civil religion. It was, we could only recognize later, a tipping point in American culture in which we were sympathetic with conservative reaffirmations of the place of Christian practice in the public sphere without yet appreciating the degree to which simplistic religion would shortly become a bad-faith alliance with power and greed. With victory in the Cold War early in the next decade

"Morning In America" ideology became a triumphalism that appeared to presage the Hegelian end to history.

A political theology of faith in technology has roots that can be traced back to the American founding. It is not just slavery and the genocide of indigenous peoples that were present from the beginning but the principled acting out of a commitment to "the conquest of nature for the relief of man's estate." One can trace a direct line of enacting belief from Francis Bacon's vision of a *New Atlantis* (1627) to John Winthrop's "City on a Hill" sermon (1630), the U.S. Constitution's tasking of Congress with power "To promote the Progress of Science and useful Arts" (1787, Article 1, section 8), and founding father and first Treasury Secretary Alexander Hamilton's "Report on Manufactures" (1791). A principled commitment to engineering and technology is even more clearly stated during the second founding in Abraham Lincoln's "Lecture on Discoveries and Inventions" (1858), which begins:

> All creation is a mine, and every man, a miner.
>
> The whole earth, and all within it, upon it, and round about it, including himself, in his physical, moral, and intellectual nature, and his susceptabilities, are the infinitely various "leads" from which, man, from the first, was to dig out his destiny.
>
> In the beginning, the mine was unopened, and the miner stood naked, and knowledgeless, upon it.
>
> Fishes, birds, beasts, and creeping things, are not miners, but feeders and lodgers, merely. Beavers build houses; but they build them in nowise differently, or better now, than they did, five thousand years ago. Ants, and honey-bees, provide food for winter; but just in the same way they did, when Solomon referred the sluggard to them as patterns of prudence.[1]

In the decades post-World War II this technological imperative began to mushroom into a universal and homogenous consumerism: from material goods to services and the synthetic freedoms of marketed experiences. Culture was sucked into a vortex of globalizing capitalism enabled by innovative engineering and technology. Media megachurches would turn platformed evangelism into prosperity gospel celebrations of excess. Only on the margins, only slightly more in Europe than America, was there any serious questioning. Our aim was, insofar as we might be able and at least for ourselves, to bring that theological questioning out of the shadows.

1. Lincoln, "First Lecture."

As Jim and I wrote in the preface, our emerging awareness of the theological-political problem of technology was follow-on to a philosophical-political one. Philosophical discourse on technology had equally been pushed aside in both the academic politics of analytic philosophy and the public political dismissal of philosophy itself. In the 1960s there had been a moment of questioning focused on nuclear weapons and environmental pollution which, in the 1970s, a previous collection on philosophy and technology had attempted to thematize and advance. It was a nascent effort to imitate what Cicero described as Socrates's practice of drawing philosophy down from a heavenly epistemology of science to dwell in the cities among human all too human things: inquiring into what is noble and base, what is moderation and madness, what is just and unjust in human affairs under conditions of engineered and engineering existence.

The implicit argument of *Philosophy and Technology* (1972) was that an inordinate engagement with engineering and technology at the very least deserved analytic observation in extra-historical and sociological terms, and perhaps even subjected to ethical-political critique. That effort in critical observation included, along with sections on conceptual, ethical-political, existential, and metaphysical issues, another on religious critiques (although Robert Mackey, my co-editor of that volume, questioned whether such discourse was genuinely philosophical). My own growing intuition of the significance of religion as a potential for moderating the engineering juggernaut led me to join the Catholic Church, as the most immediately available tradition within which to seek some small purchase on a way of life less subservient to technological imperatives.

Within the Catholic tradition I was drawn not so much to the ecclesiastical institution as to counter-movements such as the Catholic Worker and monasticism—so drawn that shortly thereafter my wife and I (with four children) joined an experimental "monastery for families." It was in the alternative intentional community of the Families of St. Benedict near the Abbey of Gethsemani in Kentucky that Jim and I met and decided to extend philosophical into more thematized theological reflection on technology. We spent five years on the project, which was only completed after the experimental family monastery unraveled and we had both returned to academic lives.

Looking back from the perspective of four decades at our attempt to engage the theological-political problem of technology, I find an argument that continues to resonate but about which I also have questions. Time and experience tend to complicate all arguments. The thesis of *Theology and Technology* was that among five ideal types of interaction between Christianity and culture—Christ in opposition, support, transcendence, paradox, or transformation—in a world in which culture has been taken over by technology, not all are equally authentic expressions of Christianity. What Christianity requires in the contemporary techno-human condition is what we called an "oppositional/dualist" stance—some creative combination of the first and fourth ideal types.

The adequacy of the typology, which was based on one by theological ethicist H. Richard Niebuhr (1951), has been questioned and extended by biblical theologian D.A. Carson (2008). After summarizing Niebuhr, criticizing him for insufficient clarity about the core doctrines of Christianity, and reviewing a suite of related discussions (including debates about postmodernism), Carson argues for analyzing Christianity in terms of four cultural forces: secularism, democracy, freedom, and power. Interestingly, he comes to a conclusion not wholly at odds with ours. Yet conspicuous by its absence is any discussion of technology, a core influence on his four forces. Carson's analysis nevertheless remains an important contribution to Christ and technological culture discourse.

In the Christ-culture discourse I would now also argue for some distinction between culture and civilization. The idea of culture implicates a kind of unconscious, closed rootedness and particularity, whereas civilization is associated with broader social orders and rationality (we speak of German *culture* but French *civilization*). We need to distinguish possibilities for Christian culture versus Christian civilization, the former exhibiting more natural tension with scientific technology than the latter.

All further analysis and reflection aside, were I still a Christian, I would continue to argue that in the techno-lifeworld of the present and foreseeable future, Christians are called to practice some form of an "oppositionist/dualist" stance. But in seeking to live that hypothesis, to take it as guidance for living practice, I came to find it also fundamentally questionable, not the least because of discovering a theology of technology that permeates not just Christianity but the Abrahamic traditions as a whole, although it is one that has been expressed with particular dominating force within a Christian ambiance.

The decisive moment for me was the September 11, 2001 Islamicist martyr terrorist attacks on the United States. For years, in saying the psalms as part of a daily, monastic-imitating office, I had struggled over the cursing psalms. Nightly at Compline we chanted Psalm 137:

> By the waters of Babylon we sat down and wept,
> when we remembered Zion.
> We hung up our lyres
> on the willows that grow in that land.
> For there our captors asked for a song,
> our tormentors called for mirth:
> "Sing us one of the songs of Zion."
> How shall we sing a song of the Lord
> on alien soil?
> If I forget thee, O Jerusalem,
> let my right hand wither.
> Let my tongue cleave to the roof of my mouth
> if I do not remember you,
> if I set not Jerusalem above my highest joy.
> Remember, O Lord, against the people of Edom
> the day of Jerusalem,
> how they said, "Down with it, down with it,
> even to the ground."
> O daughter of Babylon, doomed to destruction,
> happy is he who repays you
> for all you have done to us;
> Who takes your little ones,
> and dashes them against the rock.

There are, of course, literal, allegorical, tropological, and anagogical interpretations of these and other imprecatory texts and narrations of violence that are salted throughout the Hebrew and Greek scriptures. I tried to convince myself that they were overshadowed by other passages and teachings that called for forgiveness and love. The sense of victimhood and self-righteous anger, as well as the tradition of anathemas found not just scripture but in the long tradition of ecclesiology and rhetoric, were surely not what Friedrich Nietzsche thought: just the dark reveal of a slave morality of resentment and fanaticism. Yet as Nietzsche's interpretation was placed on global media display in a version with Islamic coloring, and I listened to all the rationalizations about how the Islamicists were not "true Muslims," any more than Christian crusaders had been "true Christians" (even though some had been canonized), something clicked.

I found myself unable to criticize Islam as a religion that nurtured fanaticism without doing the same with Christianity and Judaism.

Fanaticism and violence began to reveal themselves as deeply embedded in all three Abrahamic religions: from the demand for and willingness to murder Isaac and the divine murder of all first-born of the Egyptians to the Apocalypse of John and the cultivation of holy *jihad*. Yes, these could all be given spiritual interpretations, but such interpretations increasingly appeared to me as artificial and strained. For years I had accepted Ivan Illich's apologia for Christianity via the principle *corruptio optimi quae est pessima*; suddenly this too struck me as equally contrived. Wanting to distance myself from all Abrahamic religions I undertook a turn, first, toward the *dharma* teaching of Buddhism and, subsequently, toward the *dao* teachings of Daoism and Confucianism, in search of alternative relationships with modern technology and its distinctive secular fanaticism.

My speculative hypothesis is that on another cultural level than proposed in Lynn White Jr.'s seminal "The Historical Roots of Our Ecological Crisis" (1967)—and more politically consequential than insinuated by Martin Heidegger's ontotheological history of Being—Abrahamic religion "bears a huge burden of guilt" (better: "responsibility") for the conditions in which we find ourselves, not just theologically and politically but technologically.

Such speculation rests, of course, on a sense of our historico-philosophical condition as one of crisis that calls for Nietzschean diagnosis and therapy. Pursuing it requires, first, some stipulation of the dimensions of our civilizational crisis, politically and technologically. Prescinding from the fact that any description might well be contested, seriously entertaining such a radical thesis calls for the identification of some thread tying Abrahamic theology as theology with the distinctive character of modern politics and technology.

Studies on the origins of monotheism by Egyptologist Jan Assmann offer one entry point. In *Moses the Egyptian* (1997) and *The Price of Monotheism* (2009), Assmann explores three overlapping contrasts: religions that make no claim to universal truth versus those that do, polytheisms versus monotheisms, and primary religions versus secondary religions. The claim that one religion is true and others false, Assmann terms the "Mosaic distinction" reflecting its emphatic assertion by the traditional author of the Pentateuch and prophet of the Exodus. The Mosaic distinction is unique to monotheisms; polytheisms never make claims to universal truth but are content to function as what Assmann terms "cosmotheisms" or as indigenous cults of particular cultures. But polytheism is actually a step toward universality from "primitive ethnocentrism of tribal religions" by means of postulating functional equivalence.

> The names are, of course, different in different cultures, because the languages are different. The shapes of the gods and the forms of worship may also differ significantly. But the functions are strikingly similar, especially in the case of cosmic deities; and most deities had a cosmic function. The sun god of one religion is easily equated to the sun god of another religion, and so forth . . . . The cultures, languages, and customs may have been . . . different . . . the religions always had a common ground. Thus they functioned as a means of intercultural translatability. The gods were intercultural because they were cosmic. The different peoples worshipped different gods, but nobody contested the reality of foreign gods and the legitimacy of foreign forms of worship.[2]

Greek and Roman gods are simply Greek and Roman gods; Zeus was Jupiter and vice versa.

During the Axial Age in which they emerged in critical rejection of primary polytheisms, monotheisms can be described as secondary or counter-religions. Judaism rejected Egyptian polytheism, Christianity rejected Judaism, Islam rejected both Judaism and Christianity, in each case generating a higher degree of antagonistic energy than previously found in religious consciousness.

> The relationship between monotheistic and archaic religions is one of revolution . . . of a rupture, a break with the past that rests on the distinction between truth and falsehood and generates, over the subsequent course of its reception, the distinction between Jews and Gentiles, Christians and pagans, Christians and Jews, Muslims and infidels, true believers and heretics, manifesting itself in countless acts of violence and bloodshed.[3]

The Mosaic distinction and its antagonistic energy is infused from the claim to supernatural revelation: the one true God speaking with an authoritative command from outside the world that he has created from nothing. There is a deep contrast in antagonistic energy between monotheism and *dharma-dao* religions and their cyclical, eternal return cosmogonies that did not arrive out of nothing but at most underwent a period of divine-assisted formation by gods who were themselves part

2. Assmann, *Moses the Egyptian*, 3.
3. Assmann, *Price of Monotheism*, 11.

of the cosmos. In such circumstances a culture-religion dialectic will be unlikely to take on as radical and disruptive a form as in Judaism, Christianity, or Islam. And yet when it does disrupt, it may be likely to disrupt quite differently, as provocatively represented in the cultural memories of two warriors. When the great warrior of the Maurya Dynasty Ashoka converted to Buddhism, he abandoned warfare. When the Roman general Constantine adopted Christianity, he went into battle with *Chi Rho* painted on the shields of his solders.

My speculative hypothesis is that modern engineering and technology, as a secondary or counter-technics to craft technics, may be interpreted in terms of a claim to providing uniquely powerful methods for "directing the great Sources of Power in Nature for the use and convenience of man," to reference the 1828 definition of the British Institution of Civil Engineers. Note the presence of the definite article. There is at least a thread of analogy between the claims not just of Christianity but of all three Abrahamic religions and their world-transforming, conversion seeking dynamisms and English-speaking engineering in its modern dispensation, with its claim to uniquely effective methods for design and construction. Effectiveness and efficiency I also take to be simply polite names for power, brute power to manipulate, take charge, and transform the physical world, as exhibited through the global antagonistic exploitations of Euro-American colonial imperialism. Engineering rejects what Lewis Mumford called "polytechnics" in the name of a "monotechnics" of design and construction that will remake or "convert" the world into a universally manageable artifact in the form of a theologically political technology.

This is, of course, a thin thread. Correspondence is not causation. Yet analogy is able to stimulate reflection, can suggest ways to begin to tie together disparate aspects in the momentum of a fragmented and fragmenting, engineered and engineering civilization, promoting research that might lead to genuine insights of reflective understanding. Such is the new trajectory of theological-political thinking that has slowly emerged in my personal post *Theology and Technology* trajectory. But the real work of developing this analogy remains to be done.

To name just one example: Against the background of the argument of *Theology and Technology*, a turn away from Christianity toward Buddhism, Daoism, and Confucianism obviously raises the question of ideal typical analyses. Take Buddhism as a case in point: Could Buddhism, too, be analyzed in terms of five ideal type cultural formations: Buddha in opposition, support, transcendence, paradox, or transformation? And if so, when a culture becomes technological—when Buddhism meets technological society—can one ideal type be argued as more authentic than another? And the same goes for Daoism and Confucianism. Some contemporary discussion of the relationship between Confucianism and technology is open to interpretation within such a framework.

One hypothesis would be that the worldliness of Daoism and Confucianism (at least—Buddhism might need to be analyzed differently, though perhaps not Chinese or Mahayana Buddhism) do not exhibit the problematic dialectic of the Abrahamic religions. Both Daoism and Confucianism promote what contemporary philosopher Li Zehou (1930–2021) called a "one-world ontology." Daoism, particularly, emerged from and in continuity with shamanism, and its basic texts, from the *I Ching* and the *Laozi* to the *Zhuangzi* make no claim to be the only true texts. The *Zhuangzi* even explicitly ridicules the idea of one truth. And although early Celestial Masters in the Daoist tradition speak of receiving revelations, these are not revelations in the same radical sense of those given to Moses, present in Jesus, or spoken by Muhammed. They are, as it were, this-worldly revelations. Confucius and Confucians even more emphatically sideline other-worldly revelations.

These hypothetical speculations at present remain just that: hypothetical speculations. This modest afterword, however, is not the place to develop new arguments in any detail. For the present, and as an elucidating commentary on the standpoint of *Theology and Technology* it is perhaps sufficient to attempt to place such questions in critical reflective play.

Postscript Interview

Levi Checketts: The intellectual journey you outline in your postscript raises a number of challenging questions. Would you be willing to discuss some of them a little further?

Carl Mitcham: Of course. I continue to interrogate myself about these issues and discussion almost always opens up new things for consideration.

LC: To begin, you identify the rise of neoconservatism as having been an influence on this book, but you trace back its ideas through the American founding myth and early modernity. I'm reminded in this of how Ellul's discussion of "Technical Society" seems just a different way of talking about what Arendt calls "Mass Society" or what Marxists reduce to "capitalism." Given what you're tracing out, are these just different facets of the same phenomenon? Is the political philosophy of late modernity just a hydra (and not, contra Hobbes, a Leviathan), whose individual heads cannot be individually vanquished?

CM: It's not so much that neoconservatism was a direct influence as that, looking back now, I can see how its emergence was part of the broader historical context in which I was thinking about theology and technology. I was actually more influenced by the late, dying phase of the new left and counter-culture movements, against which neoconservatism was reacting and which it would quickly overshadow. I do see the neoconservative heroic individualist, techno-capitalist ideology (*à la* Ayn Rand) as more firmly embedded in the American experiment than progressivism or socialism of almost any type. And it is socialism of some sort that has been a consistent source for progressive criticism of technology.

As for relationships between the concepts of technical, mass, and capitalist societies: I agree that there are similarities. Ellul himself saw his study of *La Technique* as a continuation of Marx's analysis in *Das Kapital*. Arendt does a chiropractic on Marx, criticizing the masses that he saw as possessing revolutionary potential. In her own way Arendt was a contributor to neoconservatism. Arendt also exhibits some affinities with the kind of cultural conservatism that criticizes technology on essentially aesthetic grounds without proposing any progressive political reforms (see Heidegger).

The political philosophy of late modernity is indeed a hydra, but one that was, I might suggest, at least wrestled to a draw by Leo Strauss.

LC: You noted your difficulty with Psalm 137 and the "cursing psalms." Ironically, these psalms give me great comfort. When I read Psalm 137, I read the bitterness and the pain of a people vanquished by a conquering force dripping off the page. That the Judeo-Christian tradition has canonized these texts assures me that this is a tradition that faces evil. In contrast, I find Buddhism difficult because of a flight from suffering that seems to deny its reality.

CM: Your interpretation is certainly more orthodox than mine, and I tried for years to adopt it. But does any suffering, however unjust, justify cultivating an emotion of taking children and smashing their heads on rocks? Psalm 137 is not an isolated instance either. Abraham was told by God to sacrifice his young son Isaac. (I've heard sermons about the agony of Abraham about this but never about what Isaac might have been thinking.) And then God himself murdered all the first-born of the Egyptians in the process of repaying them for Hebrew bondage and suffering.

Ultimately I came to see Nietzsche's analysis of Psalm 137 as more revealing. For me these texts drip with resentment and "slave morality." For Nietzsche, "evil" (as opposed to "bad") is a counter-concept or what Freud might term a reaction formation. Buddhism, at least as I understand it, offers a more sober assessment of human suffering. Nietzsche, of course, was critical of Buddhism too.

LC: The absolutizing nature of monotheism you discuss seems to conflate some realities. Christianity, for example, formed its canon before Judaism did. And while there was certainly polemicism against the syncretic version of monotheism that the Samaritans adopted after the territory was conquered by the Assyrians, this wasn't the same thing as Christian persecution of heresy. Ironically, though, the formation of Christian dogma is inseparable from Christianity's embrace of Greek philosophical thinking. To take a very simple example, the dogmatic articulation of the Trinity, which gave rise to numerous "heresies" relies on explicitly Greek metaphysical ideas—only a perfect being can be God, a perfect thing can only be one, God is somehow three, so those three must be of one substance, etc. Indeed, as my Hebrew professor in college pointed out, the doctrine of *creatio ex nihilo*, which you highlight as absolutist, is a Christian dogma, not a Jewish one. Does this suggest the Greek insertion into Hebraic belief has more of a role in this fanaticism, or does the concordance of Greek philosophy with Christianity and Islam merely accentuate that these traditions are inherently polarizing?

CM: You raise a number of pointed difficulties here. Certainly, the relationship between Christian revelation and Greek philosophy is complex. But I don't think the distinctiveness of the Christian interpretation of revelation as anti-Jewish depended on Greek philosophy. It seems to me more that Christianity made use of Greek philosophy to more strongly express its counter-formation against Judaism, where revelation is understood as law. Law and philosophy (the questioning of law), Jerusalem and Athens, are fundamentally opposed. Christianity saw an alliance with philosophy as a way to attack Judaism—and, in the process, transformed if not corrupted philosophy.

For Assmann, the introduction of an exclusive truth claim into religious belief originated with the Egyptian pharaoh Akhenaten, from whom it was adopted by Moses and the Hebrews. Incidentally, in studies subsequent to *Moses the Egyptian* and *The Price of Monotheism*, Assmann qualifies his position, making clear he actually sees religious monotheism (as distinct from philosophical monotheism) as a cultural advance over cosmotheism. I'm not so sure myself.

Finally, with regard to the doctrine of *creatio ex nihilo*: a number of Jewish philosophers would contest the idea that this is exclusively Christian. It seems to be present in Philo of Alexandria, 2 Maccabees, and Saadia Gaon. In his interpretation of the fundamental opposition between Athens and Jerusalem, Strauss attributes the doctrine to the Hebrew Scriptures.

Incidentally, a claim for Christian canon formation prior to Jewish canon formation strikes me as depending on a contentious bias against Judaism. A Jewish view regarding the Scriptures as constituted by the TaNaKh (Torah, Prophets, and Writings) appears at least as early as Ben Sira (2nd century BCE), does it not?

LC: Rabbinic conversation about what was acceptable for the Hebrew Bible did not reach consensus until around 200 CE. You can see some of the process of disagreement between books that are included in the LXX but not the TaNaKh, often called apocryphal or deuterocanonical. Christianity, however, settled the topic much more quickly and authoritatively decades before consensus was reached in Judaism.

So you don't think the concordance of Greek philosophy with Christianity and Islam enhanced the antagonistic energy of these traditions?

CM: I think I would put it more that Christianity infused antagonistic energy into European philosophy. St. Augustine's Platonism has a more violent cast than that of Plotinus. And there is something deeply antagonistic toward the ancients in the thought of Francis Bacon and René Descartes. Bacon claims because of Christian certainty about morality we should no longer subject ethics to philosophical moderation but simply get on with the torturing of nature for the relief of man's estate; Descartes wants to introduce into philosophy a kind of secularized certainty of faith.

LC: You highlight the interconnected nature of Christian culture with "the global antagonistic exploitation of Euro-American colonial imperialism." The point is well made, but the obvious counterfactual presents itself—what about Japan? As someone with family in Korea and now living in Hong Kong, I sense still a great amount of bitterness to the violent colonialism Japan exercised a century ago across this continent.

CM: At the same time, we need to ask to what extent Japan's imperialism was influenced by or imitating the West. Japan presented its "Greater East Asian Co-Prosperity Sphere" as an alternative to Western imperialism.

LC: Good point. However, you can't deny the development of synergism between Buddhism and Bushido [way of the warrior] in Japan.

CM: Yes, and any full discussion of religious influences on Japanese violence, militarism, and the engineering of a techno-lifeworld, which Japan certainly seems to be doing, would also need to consider the role and influence of Confucianism, Daoism, and Shinto (and maybe even Christianity) in Japanese culture. While we're on Japan, I can't help but wonder about the excessive violence in manga and anime as a distinctive technology-related cultural formation.

LC: There is still the question of Korea and Hong Kong that you haven't commented on.

CM: Your knowledge of Korea and Hong Kong is so much greater than mine. I hesitate to make any comment, except an extraneous one, by noting that Korea has one of the highest investments in R&D in the world (4.55% of GDP versus 2.8% for United States) and that it is also above the OECD average (2.0%) in Japan (3.20%). I'd guess this reflects as much American military occupation and a nationalist desire to adopt a science policy of the occupier in order to free oneself from the occupier. Any discussion of religious influence on the fanatical adoption of technologies should not marginalize nationalism. I'd venture that Hong Kong is still too much under the cultural influence of more than 100 years of British imperialism to be counted as a distinctive case. (It is in part to try to correct a continuing British imperial legacy that Chairman Xi Jinping decided to take more direct control of Hong Kong.)

LC: Let me return to what I think is the primary issue. Daoism, Confucianism, and Buddhism seem to face the question of technology from a very different perspective than Christianity. Buddhism seems unconcerned about the material world at all, while Confucianism is almost exclusively focused on the material world. How they would consider "technology" as a problem seems very different, with Buddhism perhaps following something like P. Hans Sun's position (in Volume II), while Confucianism may be more similar to Paul Durbin's pragmatist approach. Do you think, though, that these religious standpoints open new questions that Christians aren't able to ask?

CM: I agree with your basic points here. My one qualification might be to caution use of the term "material world" in relation to Confucianism. I'd prefer simply "this world" or "human world" or "social world." Daoism is in a funny way more materialist: It pays more attention to the material world. Joseph Needham describes Daoism as, up until circa 1500, outpacing European science in producing empirical knowledge about the physical world. Confucianism is not properly characterized as materialist in anything like a Western sense.

As I understand it, one of the best texts for understanding Confucianism is the *Zong yong* (Doctrine of the Mean) attributed to Confucius' grandson Zisi. The *Zong yong* stresses the centrality of moderation and self-cultivation. The need for moderation could be applied especially to technology and technological change. Self-cultivation might counsel delimitation of technological and media distractions. Although I don't know of any efforts to develop such applications, there are any number of efforts by American Confucians to revive Confucian role morality as an alternative and antidote to the excessive individualism characteristic of the techno-lifeworld. See, for example, the work of and David Hall and Roger Ames.

In China, a number of philosophers have interpreted Confucianism in pragmatist terms. Recall that John Dewey spent two years in China (1919–1921), more than he spent in any country other than the United States. This was also during a period of intense Chinese cultural ferment. Other Chinese philosophers have simply decided to strike out on their own from a Confucian perspective. See, e.g., Pak-Hang Wong and Tom Xiaowei Wang, eds., *Harmonious Technology: A Confucian Ethics of Technology* (2021).

LC: But do you think these approaches raise any new questions that Christians aren't able to ask?

CM: No, of course not. The question is not whether Christians *can* ask the kinds of questions that might commonly arise in a Confucian tradition but whether they would be inclined to do so and/or whether there would be sufficient cultural energy to attempt to enact Confucian-like counsels. Over forty years ago, the Christian economist E.F. Schumacher wrote a nice paper on "Buddhist Economics" arguing for sustainable development.

LC: What about Daoism again? Daoism seems enigmatic to me on this front. On one hand, *wuwei* [principle of non-action] seems to be a strongly anti-technological principle. On the other, Hong Kong seems to combine technologies with Daoism, including, most obviously, the use of *feng shui* in designing the financial sector skyscrapers—monuments to global capitalism and Daoist sensibilities. What do you think Daoism offers on this front?

CM: Yes, Daoism is a conundrum for me as well. For some years I have been trying to learn about how Daoism might contribute to the philosophy of technology from Professor Wang Qian, a colleague at Dalian University of Technology. He and one of his students have published a short article on this topic. (See "Reflection on the Dao of Technology: Philosophy of Technology from the Perspective of Chinese Culture," in *Chinese Philosophy of Technology: Classical Readings and Contemporary Work*, 2020.) But to this point I don't feel like I have a sufficient appreciation of Daoism as a complex tradition that includes both religious teachings and philosophical ideas to understand very much. I confess to being attracted but without knowing what to make of my own attraction.

On a related note, I recommend Yuk Hui's *The Question Concerning Technology in China: An Essay in Cosmotechics* (2016) as the single most challenging work that I know. (For more detail you might see my essay review "Varieties of Technology Experience," *Issues in Science and Technology*, 2018.)

LC: You're providing a lot of references for further reading.

CM: Much of my scholarly work has been bibliographical. I've sometimes been criticized for not going further and critically engaging with all the bibliographical references I can come up with on some topic. As I age, however, I'm less up-to-date on any literature. The explosion of publications in philosophy and technology studies makes keeping up dependent on AI. (That's meant as sick joke.)

LC: As a follow-up, does the similarity between some of the approaches (such as those in Volume II by Sun or Durbin) suggest possibilities for *rapprochement* between Christianity and non-monotheistic traditions?

CM: Not sure what you mean by "rapprochement." I'm inclined to see philosophy and religion in terms of permanent alternatives or oppositions and to be suspicious of rapprochement. Think of Kant's antinomies or Derrida's *aporia*.

LC: To come full circle—it's clear that the interest of many people in the project that led to *Theology and Technology*, perhaps Jim Grote especially, was born out of the theological conviction that to be Christian is to take a prophetic stance against what we see in the present age. Such a view seems to accord with much of the development of theology through the twentieth century (e.g. liberation theology, social gospel, black theology). What is your advice for Christian theologians attempting to take up the task you began forty years ago?

CM: Being no longer a Christian, I'm uneasy offering advice to Christians. I don't think it's my place to do so. Besides, I'm still struggling to figure out what advice to give myself as a Buddhist—a not very good Buddhist, I should add, something of an unfortunately superficial Buddhist.

But I'm grateful for this opportunity to talk. Your questions are stimulating me to think and think again and will remain with me for some time. *Namo Amituofo.*

Bibliography

Assmann, Jan. *Moses the Egyptian: The Memory of Egypt in Western Monotheism.* Cambridge, MA: Harvard University Press, 1997.

———. *The Price of Monotheism.* Translated by Robert Savage. Stanford, CA: Stanford University Press, 2009.

Carson, D. A. *Christ and Culture Revisited.* Grand Rapids: William B. Eerdmans, 2008.

Hall, David L., and Roger T. Ames. *Thinking Through Confucius.* Albany, NY: SUNY Press, 1987.

Hui, Yuk. *The Question Concerning Technology in China: An Essay in Cosmotechics.* Falmouth, UK: Ubanomic, 2016.

Lincoln, Abraham. "First Lecture on Discoveries and Inventions." Speech, Bloomington, IL, April 6, 1858. Teaching American History. https://teachingamericanhistory.org/document/first-lecture-on-discoveries-and-inventions/

Mitcham, Carl. "Varieties of Technology Experience." *Issues in Science and Technology* 34, no. 4 (Summer, 2018) 89–92.

Mitcham, Carl, and Robert Mackey, eds. *Philosophy and Technology: Readings in the Philosophical Problems of Technology.* New York: Free Press, 1972.

Schumacher, E. F. "Buddhist Economics." In *Small Is Beautiful*, 56–66. New York: Harper &. Row, 1973.

Wang, Qian, and Wei Zhang. "Reflection on the Dao of Technology: Philosophy of Technology from the Perspective of Chinese Culture." In *Chinese Philosophy of Technology: Classical Readings and Contemporary Work*, edited by Qian Wang, 133–147. Singapore: Springer Nature, 2020.

Wong, Pak-Hang, and Tom Xiaowei Wang, eds. *Harmonious Technology: A Confucian Ethics of Technology.* New York: Routledge, 2021.

Conclusion

Levi Checketts

The essays in this volume and its subsequent are extensive, but by no means exhaustive. In a way, the generality of the positions here are both strength and weakness. To describe "technology" too broadly, as I argue in my own essay, runs the risk of making general conclusions that do not fit present realities or specific technologies. On the other hand, a failure to critically think about technology as a given and as having a general tendency also leads to a *de facto* tolerance of the technological imposing itself on the sacred. Within this volume, we encounter seven voices contending for one position over others on how Christians should engage with technology. Five of the essays (six, if you count Mitcham's introductory essay) were published in the original 1984 text, reflecting H. Richard Niebuhr's five ideal types with relation to the broad topic of technology. The two ending essays, my own and Mitcham's postword, engage these perspectives with over thirty years of retrospection and new perspectives, offering an evolution of thought and, perhaps a projection of what the future of this field entails. On one hand, Mitcham and I both conclude that theology shares much more in common with "technology" than has previously been considered, but on the other hand, Mitcham's assessment of this suggests Christian theology may have no real ground for challenging technology, while I conclude that the co-evolving nature of the two offers hope for what theology can offer.

Nonetheless, it is neither my nor Mitcham's interest to conclusively "resolve" this question. The following volume offers even more perspectives on the question of theology and technology, varying in the authors' assessments both of the strengths of contemporary or ancient theology and in the meaning of the technological moment we find ourselves in. And yet again, many other voices are omitted from the conversation, due to practical constraints, including the voices of major theologians and spiritual writers like Thomas Merton, C. S. Lewis, Karl Rahner, and Jürgen Moltmann. But one should never be satisfied that she has the totality of truth in her hands, and the disagreements—as well as the convergences—between various theologians over the past century or so on this topic should suggest to us the need for *more* questioning, not more answers. In this concluding section then, I offer more questions to consider—questions which I hope will prompt further conversations and research in the field, the hope I offered in my preface.

Why so many false starts, and is this a new false start?

Theological studies of technology, and ethics of technology more specifically, seems to be a very important direction for theology in the Industrial age, but despite essays, books and conferences, there is no real organization at hand for this discipline. Other sub-disciplines of theology, such as feminist theology, bioethics, postcolonial theology or eco-theology have been born from dedicated thinkers pushing for recognition in the academy. Some needs were already apparent and well-received—Catholic natural law attitudes toward fertility technologies necessitated the development of bioethics, for example. Others faced great opposition until they had successfully won the fight for inclusion, such as feminist theology, race and theology, or postcolonial theologies. For a feminist theologian like Lisa Sowle Cahill, a black liberation theologian like James Cone or a womanist theologian like M. Shawn Copeland, theological interest is inextricably intertwined with identity. If Copeland had hoped to succeed as a theologian, she would need to succeed as a black female theologian.

Technology does not occupy the same urgency, and perhaps it should not. Except for transhumanists, most moderns do not understand themselves through the primary axis of technology. Thus, theologians working on this topic can pick up the topic as an interest, but, if they find there is no audience for their work, may readily shift tracks to a more popular field. Nor does technology as a general topic occupy the same interest as biomedical technologies and procedures. Christian health care systems have a vested interested in good bioethics. But there are not Catholic engineering firms the way there are Catholic hospitals. On the other hand, as philosophers like Hans Jonas have pointed out, modern technologies pose much greater risks and demand greater accountability.[1] What are we to make of the fact that debates still rage in bioethics regarding in-vitro fertilization but similar theological interest is not found in automated systems? What should we make of some Catholic bishops' single-minded focus on abortion while technological bi-products threaten human existence on earth? How do we reconcile theological critiques of capitalism that do not reckon with the outsized influence of tech companies? The truth is technology is and always has been a critical part of theological reflection, but it too often has remained in the background.

Current interest in theological studies of technology seems promising, but it should be noted that the focus is quite narrowly applied to computing technologies and especially Artificial Intelligence (AI). The 2010s saw a massive improvement in machine learning, and the economic growth of Information and Computing Technologies companies like Microsoft, Apple, Facebook, Google and Amazon. Much of the interest in technology at present is focused on these issues, but this is a dangerous route. While AI potentially raises many critical questions, some prognosticators like STS scholar Lee Vinsel think the great leaps of AI are running out. Most interest in AI today relies on what Vinsel calls "criti-hype," commentary both supportive and critical of the technology which "hypes" up its capabilities and builds more interest in the technology than is actually warranted by the state of the art.[2]

Is Vinsel right to think that AI's time is past? If he is, theological studies of technology may experience another false start. The monied support of theological engagement with technology is largely tied to hyping up the technology. Centers for technology ethics are springing up across the world, often sponsored by large corporations like IBM's center at the University of Notre Dame, or Microsoft's center at Seattle University. In the best cases, these centers want research that helps companies make ethical choices in their technological endeavors—none question whether the technological fixation is itself the danger. At the same time, as tech companies expand their influence beyond Silicon Valley and Seattle to various metropoles across the world, and as issues of bias, economic injustice, environmental degradation and privacy invasion become more recognized, theologians in other fields will need to pay more attention to

1. Jonas, *The Imperative of Responsibility*, 11.
2. Vinsel, "You're Doing it Wrong."

technology than they have previously. Beyond ethics, biblical studies and systematic theology will at some point need to address new theological questions that Natural Language Processing and unsupervised machine learning pose. How many software engineers will claim AI is a "new god" before theologians finally explain why such claims are based in poor understandings of both AI and God?

It is, of course, quite possible that theological studies of technology experience once again another false start. Digital theology may become the dominant framework over general technological considerations. Theological studies of technology may flourish in a decentralized or unsystematized fashion. Various technologies may continue to be addressed in a merely *ad hoc* rather than systematic fashion. Who can know? The worst result, in my opinion, would be for Christian leaders to uncritically support new technologies without rigorous theological inquiry into the way the technologies fit into a thick account of the sacred. The risk of uncritical adoption seems to be latent within the projects of some well-meaning NGOs as well as some more affluent mega-church congregations. But even the most techno-optimistic Christian can see the danger of over-reliance on technologies developed devoid of critical reflection.

Which other voices should have been included?

Mitcham and Grote had to make editorial choices in whose voices they included in this work. Others certainly could have been selected. In *Philosophy and Technology*, published a decade prior, Mitcham and Robert Mackey included a number of other essays that should be read alongside these, including the thought of Nikolai Berdyaev, C. S. Lewis, W. Norris Clarke, and Lynn White, Jr.[3] Certainly many other theologians of the era could have been included as well. In my own teaching, I have supplemented the readings from this work and *Philosophy and Technology* with essays from Karl Rahner, Thomas Merton, Paul Tillich, Jürgen Moltmann, and Pierre Teilhard de Chardin.[4] Other voices that have recently gained more interest include Romano Guardini, whom Pope Francis quotes

3. Mitcham and Mackey, *Philosophy and Technology*, 203-265.

4. Essays I have used in teaching include the following: Rahner, *Theological Investigations IX*, 205-224; Merton, *Raids on the Unspeakable*; Tillich, "The Person in a Technological Society"; Moltmann, "Has Modern Society any Future?"; Teilhard de Chardin, "The Place of Technology in the General Biology of Mankind."

frequently in his encyclical on the environment *Laudato Si'*, and Ivan Illich.[5]

Aside from these voices, a number of critical perspectives are notably absent. First, all voices in this volume belong to white men. How different would the experience or perspective of theology and its fit with technology be from a person who does not occupy a hegemonic place within Christianity, whether as an ordained pastor or merely as a white male academic writing in the mid-twentieth century? Today, many women's voices are readily apparent in this field: Noreen Herzfeld, Jean Thweatt-Bates, Simone Natale, Jamie Brummitt, Elizabeth Drescher, Nadia Delicata and others have contributed greatly to contemporary theological discussions of technology.[6] Many people of color also are making headway into this area, including Philip Butler, Nona Jones, Pauline Hope Cheong, Luis Vera and others.[7] Perhaps most exciting is the fact that theological studies of technology is also beginning to gain traction in other countries beyond anglophone and European nations, including India, South Korea, Japan and elsewhere. An example of just such a confluence of gender, race and geography is found in Agnes Brazal and Kochurani Abraham's edited volume *Feminist Cyberethics in Asia*. The location of these voices and their critical distances from the center provide new opportunities and new understandings of the confluence of faith and technology in a world that is increasingly understanding itself outside of a narrow window of white male voices.

Finally, the nebulousness of the discipline itself invites extra-disciplinary voices as well. Mitcham and Albert Borgmann, both of whom have contributed invaluably to shaping theological studies of technology, are better known for their work in philosophy. We might also add STS scholars, whose dedicated study of technology can give theologians better perspective than the ordinary methods of theology provide. John Staudenmaier, SJ, for example, is an historian of technology whose work

5. See, e.g., Guardini, *The End of the Modern World*; and Illich, *Tools for Conviviality*. Pope Francis cites Guardini nine times in his encyclical, more times than any non-scriptural authority, including Thomas Aquinas.

6. See, e.g., Herzfeld, *In Our Image*; Thweatt-Bates, *Cyborg Selves*; Natale, *Deceitful Media*; Brummitt, "Sacred Relics of To-morrow"; Drescher, *Tweet if You Heart Jesus*; and Delicata, "*Homo technologicus*."

7. See, e.g., Butler, *Black Transhuman Liberation Theology*; Jones, *From Social Media to Social Ministry*; Cheong, "Bounded Religious Automation at Work"; Vera, "Augmented Reality."

at times ventures into reflections on the development of theology,[8] and Actor-Network Theorist Bruno Latour has written about the (dis)connection of faith and technology as well.[9] We might also include voices from communications and media studies, such as Walter Ong or Paul Soukup.[10] The future of theological studies of technology, as is true of its origin, will inevitably be interdisciplinary. As theologians converse with and study work done in these and other fields, they will not only be able to better articulate the theological relevance of new technologies but also to make theology relevant for non-theological disciplines.

A full reader for theological studies of technology should include all these perspectives and more. The task of creating accessible yet extensive collections is in dire need. A full picture of where the field has been, where it is now, what is occurring at present, and where it might go is lacking. Such a project is of great need, and, I think, interest. The strengths, but more importantly the lacks of this book should inspire renewed interest in foundational questions of theological studies of technology. After all, without the voices of the majority of Christians (women generally, LGBTQ people, persons of color, non-Western thinkers), and without expanded studies of religion and technology, what remains is a very narrow image indeed of what is theologically relevant about technology. The dialogue must be expanded, and the voices of others not present here must be given equal footing.

Which religious voices have not been heard?

With perhaps the exception of Mitcham's new essay, this text is exclusively Christian in its orientation. Unlike the lack of sexual and racial diversity, this is intentional, but it does represent a limitation. The term "theology" suffers from a fair amount of ambiguity that should be noted. Sacred Theology or dogmatic theology is a uniquely Christian, specifically doctrinal area of work. Within this field, heterodoxy and orthodoxy receive clear definitions. The essays of this work do not properly constitute this area of thought since they make no claim (nor should they) about who God is. This is also why the phrase "theology of technology" is an erroneous

8. E.g., Staudenmaier, "Electric Lights Cast Long Shadows."

9. Latour, "'Thou Shall Not Freeze-Frame.'"

10. E.g. Soukup, *Communication and Theology*. The writings of Ong are well enough noted in this volume, e.g. Fudpucker's essay.

construction—theology is always about God. In a less strict sense, however, theology is, in the words of Anselm of Canterbury, "faith seeking understanding." In this sense, theology remains Christian, as the content of Christian faith and its deposit are worked out into intelligible formulations. It is this second sense where the present work finds its bearing and situates itself. Finally, a much looser sense of theology, (much looser than the senses Sun discusses in his essay in the next volume), is merely "God-talk" (*Theos-Logos*), which can then include non-Christian traditions such as Judaism or Islam. This sense of theology is confusing, however, since theologians working in a Christian seminary are bound by constraints of orthodoxy that a Jewish theologian working in a religious studies department would not experience. To avoid confusion, this work focuses on Christian theology (in the second sense), but an interreligious reader on technology is long overdue. Mitcham's retrospective essay provides an entrée for the comparative theologian or religious scholar who wishes to consider the place of Christian theological study of technology alongside Daoist, Confucian or Buddhist reflections.

Within the realm of Christian theological studies of technology (here one might note the descriptive becomes longer with the recognition of the limitations of our work), we can note that different views correspond to different denominations or orders. Recent work in Evangelical theology, for example, is less critical of technology generally. Some of the NGOs mentioned in the preface, FaithTech and TheoTech most specifically, are Evangelical organizations that see technology as a tool for evangelizing. We might also note how "pro-technology" the Society of Jesus tends to be, as evidenced by the contributions in this area from Walter Ong, W. Norris Clarke, Pierre Teilhard de Chardin, Karl Rahner, Bernard Lonergan and contemporary Jesuits like Paul Soukup, Antonio Spadaro, Timothy Clancy and John Staudenmaier. The Jesuit slogan *Ad Maiorem Dei Gloriam* seems to sum up their attitude toward technology: ordered "to the greater glory of God," it is a worthwhile pursuit.

Aside from these positions, however, most denominations and religious orders seem to not have a strong attitude toward technology. Reformed theology, for example, includes the techno-skepticism of the field's most famous author, Jacques Ellul, along with George Grant but also those who cautiously support transformation of technology like Schuurman and Moltmann. Lutheranism likewise includes two of the more senior theologians working on science and technology today, Ted Peters and Philip Hefner, but also Paul Tillich's caution against being swept into the technological mode. Catholicism more broadly, once one gets outside the Society of Jesus, has strong critics in Thomas Merton, Albert Borgmann, and Ivan Illich.

What does this tell us? Most Christian religious groupings, with notable outliers, do not have a strong theological posture toward new technologies. Evangelicals and the Amish show up as the extremes. Evangelicals have appropriated nearly every technology of the information age in their ministry, from radio to tv, to the Internet and now Big Data analytics.[11] The Amish, on the other hand, live with a principled rejection of industrial technology, opting for tools that do not require mechanical power to do their work. Between these two poles, every other Christian denomination seems to sit, with some having more pronounced positions, and others less, but all being generally a mix of pro and contra attitudes.

More significantly, though, this suggests the need for *more* theological reflection on new technologies. While many Catholic bioethicists may lament magisterial positions on fertility technologies, there is room to dialogue about these. If there were no just war tradition, could Christians articulate a clear response to the threat of nuclear weapons? It is not a coincidence that the Catholic Church's lack of a clear labor theology preceding the Industrial Era corresponds to the relative lateness of the first magisterial response to capitalism (1891) compared to the first economic articulation of capitalism (1776). What a pontifical or synodal response to new technologies would look like is unclear, but the lack of such a response to the present suggests Christian leaders have not yet taken seriously the challenge of new and developing technologies.

Call to action

It is this lack that needs to be addressed. We see that the seeds are planted and many of the present needs for the field have been laid out. What is needed now is engagement of scholarship. A dozen or so books will come out this year and the next about various technologies—mostly digital and many of them on AI. How many will grapple seriously with the thought of theologians from the past century? How many of them will engage with the theoretical insights and limitations of Ellul or Malet or

11. Safdar, "Churches Target New Members."

Mitcham? How many of them will acknowledge the path they are treading and whose shoulders they stand upon?

If theological studies of technology is not to be stillborn once again, the scholars who read this and those already working in the field must learn to dialogue, must build from each other and must engage their work with epistemic humility. Can a Society for Theology and Technology emerge? Will there be a renewal of the *Journal of Religion, Theology and Technology*? Will scholars draft sample reading lists and syllabi to share for the classes they teach? Will centers of technology ethics collect resources of critical voices rather than just supportive voices? Will the next generations of scholars be adequately trained to talk about the history and direction of theological studies of technology rather than merely attempting to reinvent the wheel each time?

How we answer these questions will determine what is to happen. If the timing is wrong, if the interest in the field lacks, if the scholars working now pay no attention to the foundations, or if there is not coinciding institutional support, it may never come. Perhaps theological studies of technology is destined to forever remain fragmented, with a portion devoted to missiology, another portion to pedagogy, a further one found in biomedical ethics, and another in just war thought. If that happens, at the very least, this reprinting will make it easier for some reader who wants to revisit these now-classic essays. But it is my hope that the project is worthwhile, and that the reflections of theologians from the past century can inspire constructive directions for a field whose importance has never been clearer.

Bibliography

Brazal, Agnes, and Kochurani Abraham, eds. *Feminist Cyberethics in Asia: Religious Discourses on Human Connectivity*. New York: Palgrave MacMillan, 2014.

Brummitt, Jamie L. "'Sacred Relics of To-morrow': The Presence of Protestant Relics in the Mid-Nineteenth-Century Ohio Valley." *Ohio Valley History* 20, no. 4 (Winter 2020) 8–32.

Butler, Philip. *Black Transhuman Liberation Theology: Technology and Spirituality*. London: Bloomsbury, 2019.

Cheong, Pauline Hope. "Bounded Religious Automation at Work: Communicating Human Authority in Artificial Intelligence Networks." *Journal of Communication Inquiry* 45, no. 1 (2021) 5–23.

Delicata, Nadia. "*Homo technologicus* and the Recovery of a Universal Ethic: Maximus the Confessor and Romano Guardini." *Scientia et Fides* 6, no. 2 (2018) 33–53.

Drescher, Elizabeth. *Tweet if You Heart Jesus: Practicing Church in the Digital reformation*. New York: Morehouse Publishing, 2011.

Guardini, Romano. *The End of the Modern World*. Translated by Joseph Theman and Herbert Burke. Wilmington, DE: ISI Books, 1998.

Herzfeld, Noreen L. *In Our Image: Artificial Intelligence and the Human Spirit*. Minneapolis: Augsburg Fortress, 2002.

Illich, Ivan. *Tools for Conviviality*. New York: Harper&Row, 1973.

Jonas, Hans. *The Imperative of Responsibility: In Search of an Ethics for the Technological Age*. Translated by Hans Jonas and David Herr. Chicago: University of Chicago Press, 1984.

Jones, Nona. *From Social Media to Social Ministry: A Guide to Digital Discipleship*. Grand Rapids: Zondervan Reflective, 2020.

Latour, Bruno. "'Thou Shall Not Freeze Frame' or How Not to Misunderstand the Science and Religion Debate." In *Science, Religion, and the Human Experience*, edited by James D. Proctor, 27-48. Oxford: Oxford University Press, 2005.

Merton, Thomas. *Raids on the Unspeakable*. New York: New Directions, 1964.

Mitcham, Carl, and Robert Mackey, eds. *Philosophy and Technology: Readings in the Philosophical Problems of Technology*. New York: Free Press, 1972.

Moltmann, Jürgen. "Has Modern Society any Future?" In *Faith and the Future: Essays on Theology, Solidarity and Modernity*, 167–177. Maryknoll, NY: Orbis Books, 1995.

Natale, Simone. *Deceitful Media: Artificial Intelligence and Social Life after the Turing Test*. Oxford: Oxford University Press, 2021.

Rahner, Karl. *Theological Investigations IX: Writings of 1965–67*. Translated by Graham Harrison. New York: Herder & Herder, 1972.

Safdar, Khadeeja. "Churches Target New Members with Help from Big Data." *The Wall Street Journal*. December 26, 2021.

Soukup, Paul. *Communication and Theology: Introduction and Review of the Literature*. London: World Association for Christian Communication, 1983.

Staudenmaier, John. "Electric Lights Cast Long Shadows: Seeking the Greater Good in a World of Competing Clarities." *Boardman Lecture in Christian Ethics* 7. Philadelphia: University of Pennsylvania Press, 2005.

Teilhard de Chardin, Pierre. "The Place of Technology in a General Biology of Mankind." In *Activation of Energy*, translated by René Hague, 153–163. San Diego: Harcourt, 1978.

Thweatt-Bates, Jeanine. *Cyborg Selves: A Theological Anthropology of the Posthuman*. Farnham, UK: Ashgate, 2012.

Tillich, Paul. "The Place of the Person in a Technological Society." In *Social Ethics: Issues in Ethics and Society*, edited by Gibson Winter, 120–38. London: SCM Press, 1968.

Vera, Luis. "Augmented Reality and the Limited Promise of 'Eschatological' Technology Criticism." *Journal of Moral Theology* 9, no. 2 (2020) 147–174.

Vinsel, Lee. "You're Doing It Wrong: Notes on Criticism and Technology Hype." *STS News*. February 2, 2021. https://sts-news.medium.com/youre-doing-it-wrong-notes-on-criticism-and-technology-hype-18b08b4307e5

Bibliography

Ajemian, Robert. "Zealous Lord of a Vast Domain." *Time*, March 30, 1981.

Anderson, William H. U., ed. *Theology and Technology*. Wilmington, DE: Vernon Press, 2021.

Assmann, Jan. *Moses the Egyptian: The Memory of Egypt in Western Monotheism*. Cambridge, MA: Harvard University Press, 1997.

———. *The Price of Monotheism*. Translated by Robert Savage. Stanford, CA: Stanford University Press, 2009.

Barbour, Ian. *Ethics in an Age of Technology*. San Francisco: HarperCollins, 1993.

Berger, Peter L. *A Rumor of Angels*. Garden City, NY: Doubleday Anchor, 1970.

———. *The Sacred Canopy: Elements of a Sociological Theory of Religion*. Garden City, NY: Doubleday Anchor, 1968.

Bindewald, Andrée "Technology and Man's Future: Integrating Body and Spirit." *Humanitas* 14, no. 1 (February 1978) 31–46.

Blair, George A. "The Meaning of 'Energia' and 'Entelechia' in Aristotle." *International Philosophical Quarterly* 7, no. 1 (March 1967) 101–117.

Boomershine, Thomas. "The Embodiment of the Word: A Pastoral Approach to Scripture in a Digital Age." *Communications Research Trends* 37, no. 2 (2018) 15–19.

Borgmann, Albert. *Power Failure: Christianity in the Culture of Technology*. Grand Rapids: Brazos Press, 2003.

Brazal, Agnes, and Kochurani Abraham, eds. *Feminist Cyberethics in Asia: Religious Discourses on Human Connectivity*. New York: Palgrave MacMillan, 2014.

Brummitt, Jamie L. "'Sacred Relics of To-morrow': The Presence of Protestant Relics in the Mid-Nineteenth-Century Ohio Valley." *Ohio Valley History* 20, no. 4 (Winter 2020) 8–32.

Buswell, Robert E., and Timothy S. Lee. *Christianity in Korea*. Honolulu: University of Hawai'i, 2006.

Butler, Philip. *Black Transhuman Liberation Theology: Technology and Spirituality*. London: Bloomsbury, 2019.

Calvin, John. *Institutes of the Christian Religion*. Translated by Henry Beveridge. Orlando: Signalman, 2009.

Carson, D. A. *Christ and Culture Revisited*. Grand Rapids: William B. Eerdmans, 2008.

Checketts, Levi. "The Sacrality of Things: On the Technological Augmentation of the Sacred." *Techné: Research in Philosophy and Technology* 25, No. 1 (2021) 130–152.

———. "The Cross and the Computer: Actor-Network Theory and Christianity." *Theology and Science* 15, no. 1 (January 2017) 16–27.

Cheong, Pauline Hope. "Bounded Religious Automation at Work: Communicating Human Authority in Artificial Intelligence Networks." *Journal of Communication Inquiry* 45, no. 1 (2021) 5–23.

Clarke, W. Norris. "Technology and Man: A Christian View." In *Philosophy and Technology Readings in the Philosophical Problems of Technology*, edited by Carl Mitcham and Robert Mackey, 247–258. New York: The Free Press, 1972.

Clossey, Luke. *Salvation and Globalization in the Early Jesuit Missions*. Cambridge: Cambridge University Press, 2008.

Cox, Harvey G. *Feast of Fools*. Cambridge, MA: Harvard University Press, 1969.

———. *The Secular City*. New York: Macmillan, 1965.

Crofts, Richard A. "Printing, Reform, and the Catholic Reformation in Germany (1521–1545)." *Sixteenth Century Journal* 16, no. 3 (1985) 369–381.

Delicata, Nadia. "*Homo technologicus* and the Recovery of a Universal Ethic: Maximus the Confessor and Romano Guardini." *Scientia et Fides* 6, no. 2 (2018) 33–53.

Dessauer, Friederich. *Philosphie der Technick*. Bonn: Ernst Klett Verlag, 1927.

Drescher, Elizabeth. "Pixels Perpetual Shine: The Mediation of Illness, Dying and Death in the Digital Age." *CrossCurrents* 62, no. 2 (2012) 204–218.

———. *Tweet if You Heart Jesus: Practicing Church in the Digital reformation*. New York: Morehouse Publishing, 2011.

Dupuy, Jean-Pierre. *The Mark of the Sacred*. Translated by M. B. Debevoise. Stanford: Stanford University Press, 2013.

Durkheim, Emile. *The Elementary Forms of the Religious Life*. Translated by Joseph Ward Swain. London: George Allen &Unwin, 1964.

Eliade, Mircea. *The Sacred and the Profane*. New York: Harcourt Brace & World, 1959.

Ellul, Jacques. *Ethics of Freedom*. Grand Rapids, MI: Eerdmans, 1976.

———. "Nature, Technique and Artificiality." *Research in Philosophy and Technology* 3 (1980) 263–283.

———. *The Technological Society*. Translated by John Wilkinson. New York: Vintage Books, 1964.

Faramelli, Norman J. *Technethics: Christian Mission in an Age of Technology*. New York: Friendship Press, 1971.

Foucault, Michel. *Discipline and Punish: The Birth of the Prison*. Translated by Alan Sheridan. New York: Vintage Books, 1995.

Gibson, Arthur. "Visions of the Future." In *Humanism and Christianity*, edited by Claude Geffre, 118–126. New York: Herder & Herder, 1973.

Graham, Mark. "Technology and the Catholic Ethic of Use: Starting a New Conversation." *Journal of Religion, Theology and Technology* 3, no. 1 (November 2012) 1–21.

Guardini, Romano. *The End of the Modern World*. Translated by Joseph Theman and Herbert Burke. Wilmington, DE: ISI Books, 1998.

Gustafson, James M. "Christian Attitudes toward a Technological Society." *Theology Today* 16, no. 2 (July 1959) 173–187.

Hall, David L., and Roger T. Ames. *Thinking Through Confucius*. Albany, NY: SUNY Press, 1987.

Happold, F. C. *Mysticism: A Study and an Anthology*. Baltimore: Penguin, 1970.

Hefner, Philip. *Technology and Human Becoming*. Minneapolis: Fortress Press, 2003.

Hegel, Georg Wilhelm Friedrich. *The Philosophy of History*. Translated by J. Sibree. New York: Dover, 1956.

Heidegger, Martin. "Hölderlin and the Essence of Poetry." In *The Heidegger Reader*, edited by Günter Figal, translated by Jerome Veith, 117–129. Bloomington: Indiana University Press, 2007.

———. *The Question Concerning Technology and Other Essays*. Translated by William Lovitt. New York: Harper & Row, 1977.

Heilbroner, Robert L. *An Inquiry into the Human Prospect*. New York: W. W. Norton, 1974.

Hengel, Martin. *Crucifixion*. Translated by John Bowden. Philadelphia: Fortress Press, 1977.

Herzfeld, Noreen L. *In Our Image: Artificial Intelligence and the Human Spirit*. Minneapolis: Augsburg Fortress, 2002.

Holborn, Louise W. "Printing and the Growth of a Protestant Movement in Germany from 1517 to 1524." *Church History* 11, no. 2 (1942) 123–137.

Hughes, Philip John. "Dishonour, Degradation and Display: Crucifixion in the Roman World." *Harts and Minds: The Journal for Humanities and Arts* 1, no. 3 (2013) 1–24.

Hugo, Victor. "Saison des Semailles." In *Les Chansons des Rues et de Bois*, 231. Paris: Libraire Internationale, 1865.

Hui, Yuk. *The Question Concerning Technology in China: An Essay in Cosmotechics*. Falmouth, UK: Ubanomic, 2016.

Illich, Ivan. *Tools for Conviviality*. New York: Harper&Row, 1973.

Jonas, Hans. "Change and Permanence: On the Possibility of Understanding History." In *Philosophical Essays: From Ancient Creed to Modern Man*, 240–263. New York: Atropos Press, 2010.

———. *The Imperative of Responsibility: In Search of an Ethics for the Technological Age*. Translated by Hans Jonas and David Herr. Chicago: University of Chicago Press, 1984.

Jones, Nona. *From Social Media to Social Ministry: A Guide to Digital Discipleship*. Grand Rapids: Zondervan Reflective, 2020.

Joyce, James. *A Portrait of the Artist as a Young Man*. New York: Viking, 1964.

Jünger, Ernst. *Storm of Steel*. Garden City, NY: Doubleday, 1929.

Kelber, Werner H. "Walter Ong's Three Incarnations of the Word: Orality, Literacy, Technology." *Philosophy Today* 23, no. 1 (Spring 1979) 70–74.

Koyré, Alexandre. "Dur Monde de l'à Peu Près a l'Univers de la Precision." *Critique* 4, no. 28 (September 1948) 806–823.

Latour, Bruno. *Reassembling the Social: An Introduction to Actor-Network-Theory*. Oxford: Oxford University Press, 2005.

———. "'Thou Shall Not Freeze Frame' or How Not to Misunderstand the Science and Religion Debate." In *Science, Religion, and the Human Experience*, edited by James D. Proctor, 27-48. Oxford: Oxford University Press, 2005.

Lincoln, Abraham. "First Lecture on Discoveries and Inventions." Speech, Bloomington, IL, April 6, 1858. Teaching American History. https://teachingamericanhistory.org/document/first-lecture-on-discoveries-and-inventions/

Lonergan, Bernard. *Bernard Lonergan: 3 Lectures*. Montreal: Thomas More Institute for Adult Education, 1975.

———. *Collection: Papers by Bernard Lonergan*. Edited by F. Crowe. New York: Herder & Herder, 1967.

———. *Insight: A Study of Human Understanding*. Revised students' edition. New York: Philosophical Library, 1958.

———. *Method in Theology*. New York: Herder & Herder, 1972.

———. "The Ongoing Genesis of Methods." *Studies in Religion/Sciences Religieuses* 6, no. 4 (1976–1977) 341–355.

———. *Philosophy of God, and Theology*. Philadelphia: Westminster Press, 1973.

———. *A Second Collection*. Edited by W. Ryan and B. Tyrrell. Philadelphia: Westminster Press, 1974.

———. *Verbum: Word and Idea in Aquinas*. Edited by David Burrell. Notre Dame: University of Notre Dame Press, 1967.

Luther, Martin. *Commentary on Romans*. Luther's Works 25. St Louis: Concordia, 1972.

———. *An Open Letter on the Harsh Book Against the Peasants*. Luther's Works 46. Philadelphia: Fortress, 1967.

Lyons, Dan. "Are Luddites Confused?" *Inquiry* 22, No. 4 (Winter 1979) 381–403.

Malet, André. "Le Croyant en face de la technique." *Revue d'Histoire et de Philosophie Religieuses* 55, No. 3 (1975) 417–430.

Maritain, Jacques. *Integral Humanism: Temporal and Spiritual Problems of a New Christendom*. Translated by Joseph W. Evans. New York: Scribner, 1968.

———. *On the Philosophy of History*. Edited by Joseph Owens. New York: Scribner, 1957.

———. *The Rights of Man and Natural Law*. Translated by Doris C. Anson. New York: Scribner, 1943.

———. *Theonas*. Translated by F. J. Sheed. New York: Sheed & Ward, 1933.

Merton, Thomas. *Raids on the Unspeakable*. New York: New Directions, 1964.

Mitcham, Carl. "The Love of Technology is the Root of All Evils." *Epiphany* 8, no. 1 (1987) 17–28.

———. "Religion and Technology." In *A Companion to the Philosophy of Technology*, edited by Jan Kyrre Berg Olsen et al., 466–473. Malden, MA: Wiley-Blackwell, 2009.

———. "Varieties of Technology Experience." *Issues in Science and Technology* 34, no. 4 (Summer, 2018) 89–92.

Mitcham, Carl, and Robert Mackey, eds. *Philosophy and Technology: Readings in the Philosophical Problems of Technology*. New York: Free Press, 1972.

Mitchell, Nathan D. "Ritual and New Media." *Concilium* 2005, no. 1 (2005) 90–98.

Moltmann, Jürgen. "Has Modern Society any Future?" In *Faith and the Future: Essays on Theology, Solidarity and Modernity*, 167–177. Maryknoll, NY: Orbis Books, 1995.

de la Motte, Antoine Houdar. "L'Academi des Sciences." In *Oeuvres I*, 95–99. Paris: Prault, 1754.

Mounier, Emmanuel. *Be Not Afraid: A Denunciation of Despair*. London: Rockliff, 1951.

Natale, Simone. *Deceitful Media: Artificial Intelligence and Social Life after the Turing Test*. Oxford: Oxford University Press, 2021.

Niebuhr, H. Richard. *Christ and Culture*. New York: Harper & Row, 1951.

Nogar, Raymond J., OP. *The Lord of the Absurd*. New York: Herder & Herder, 1966.

Ong, Walter J. *American Catholic Crossroads: Religious-Secular Encounters in the Modern World*. New York: Macmillan, 1959.

———. *The Barbarian Within, and Other Fugitive Essays and Studies.* New York, Macmillan, 1962.
———. "The Challenge of Technology." *Sign*, February 1968. 21–24.
———. "Christian Values at Mid-Twentieth Century." *Theology Digest* 4, no. 3 (Autumn 1956) 155–157.
———. *Frontiers in American Catholicism.* New York: Macmillan, 1957.
———. *In the Human Grain.* New York: Macmillan, 1967.
———. *Interfaces of the Word: Studies in the Evolution of Consciousness and Culture.* Ithaca: Cornell University Press, 1977.
———. *Ramus, Method, and the Decay of Dialogue.* Cambridge, MA: Harvard University Press, 1958.
———. *Ramus and Talon Inventory.* Cambridge, MA: Harvard University Press, 1958.
———. "The Spiritual Meaning of Technology and Culture" In *Technology and Culture in Perspective*, edited by Myron B. Bloy, Jr. and Ilene Montana, 29-34. Cambridge, MA: Church Society for College Work, 1967.
Pascal, Blaise. *Pensées.* Edited by Léon Brunschvicg. Lutetia Edition. Paris: Classiques Français, 1949.
Paul VI. *Sacrosancturn Concilium.* Vatican City: Libreria Editrice Vaticana, 1963.
———. *Dei Verbum.* Vatican City: Libreria Editrice Vaticana, 1965.
Pinch, Trevor, Malcolm Ashmore, and Michael Mulkay. "Technology, Testing, Text: Clinical Budgeting in the U.K. National Health Service." In *Shaping Technology/ Building Society: Studies in Sociotechnical Change*, edited by Wiebe E. Bijker and John Law, 265–289. Cambridge, MA: MIT Press, 1992.
Rahner, Karl. *Theological Investigations VIII.* New York: Herder & Herder, 1972.
———. *Theological Investigations IX: Writings of 1965–67.* Translated by Graham Harrison. New York: Herder & Herder, 1972.
———. *Zur Theologie der Zukunft.* Munich: Deutscher Taschenbuch, 1971.
Rauschenbusch, Walter. *A Theology for the Social Gospel.* New York: Cosimo Classics, 2012.
Safdar, Khadeeja. "Churches Target New Members with Help from Big Data." *The Wall Street Journal.* December 26, 2021.
Schreiber, Mathias. "Deutsche for Sale." *Der Spiegel* 40 (2006) 182–198.
Schumacher, E. F. "Buddhist Economics." In *Small Is Beautiful*, 56–66. New York: Harper &. Row, 1973.
Schuurman, Egbert. *Technology in a Christian-Philosophical Perspective.* Transvaal, South Africa: Potchefstroom University, 1980.
———. *Technology and the Future: A Philosophical Challenge* (Toronto: Wedge, 1980).
Soukup, Paul. *Communication and Theology: Introduction and Review of the Literature.* London: World Association for Christian Communication, 1983.
Spadaro, Antonio. *Friending God: Social Media, Spirituality and Community.* Translated by Robert H. Hopcke. Chestnut Ridge, NY: Crossroad Publishing, 2016.
Staudenmaier, John. "Electric Lights Cast Long Shadows: Seeking the Greater Good in a World of Competing Clarities." *Boardman Lecture in Christian Ethics* 7. Philadelphia: University of Pennsylvania Press, 2005.
Taylor, Charles. *A Secular Age.* Cambridge, MA: Belknap Press, 2007.
Teilhard de Chardin, Pierre. *The Divine Milieu.* New York: Harper & Row, 1960.
———. *The Making of a Mind: Letters from a Soldier-Priest 1914–1919.* New York: Harper & Row, 1965.

———. “On Looking at a Cyclotron.” In *Activation of Energy*, translated by René Hague, 347–358. San Diego: Harcourt, 1978.

———. *The Phenomenon of Man*. Translated by Bernard Wall. New York: Harper & Row, 1959.

———. “The Place of Technology in a General Biology of Mankind.” In *Activation of Energy*, translated by René Hague, 153–163. San Diego: Harcourt, 1978.

———. “Some Reflections on the Spiritual Repercussions of the Atom Bomb.” In *The Future of Man*, translated by Norman Denny, 133–142. New York: Doubleday, 1964.

———. “Teilhard de Chardin’s Thought as Written by Himself.” In *Teilhard de Chardin: The Man and His Theories*, by Abbé Paul Grenet, 148–149. New York: Paul S. Erikson, 1966.

Thweatt-Bates, Jeanine. *Cyborg Selves: A Theological Anthropology of the Posthuman*. Farnham, UK: Ashgate, 2012.

Tillich, Paul. “The Place of the Person in a Technological Society.” In *Social Ethics: Issues in Ethics and Society*, edited by Gibson Winter, 120–38. London: SCM Press, 1968.

———. *The Spiritual Situation in Our Technical Society*. Macon, GA: Mercer University Press, 1988.

Tillotson, John. *An Answer to Discourse against Transubstantiation*. London: Henry Mills, 1687.

Vera, Luis. “Augmented Reality and the Limited Promise of ‘Eschatological’ Technology Criticism.” *Journal of Moral Theology* 9, no. 2 (2020) 147–174.

Verbeek, Peter-Paul. *What Things Do: Philosophical Reflections on Technology, Agency and Design*. Translated by Robert P. Crease. University Park, PA: Pennsylvania State University, 2000.

Vinsel, Lee. “You’re Doing It Wrong: Notes on Criticism and Technology Hype.” *STS News*. February 2, 2021. https://sts-news.medium.com/youre-doing-it-wrong-notes-on-criticism-and-technology-hype-18b08b4307e5

Wang, Qian, and Wei Zhang. “Reflection on the Dao of Technology: Philosophy of Technology from the Perspective of Chinese Culture.” In *Chinese Philosophy of Technology: Classical Readings and Contemporary Work*, edited by Qian Wang, 133–147. Singapore: Springer Nature, 2020.

Wells, H. G. *Men Like Gods*. E-book edition. Adelaide: University of Adelaide, 2014.

Wesley, John. “Sermon CXVI.” In *Works of John Wesley*, 7:##–##. Grand Rapids, MI: Zondervan, 1872.

White, Lynn, Jr. “Continuing the Conversation.” In *Western Man and Environmental Ethics*, edited by Ian G. Barbour, 55–64. Reading, MA: Addison-Wesley, 1973.

———. *Machina Ex Deo: Essays in the Dynamism of Western Culture*. Cambridge, MA: MIT Press, 1968.

———. *Medieval Religion and Technology: Collected Essays*. Berkeley: University of California Press, 1978.

———. *Medieval Technology of Social Change*. New York: Oxford University Press, 1962.

Wong, Pak-Hang, and Tom Xiaowei Wang, eds. *Harmonious Technology: A Confucian Ethics of Technology*. New York: Routledge, 2021.

Index

Made in the USA
Coppell, TX
16 May 2023